Penguin Grammar Workbook 3 Intermediate

Tim Kelly

Series Editor: Edward Woods

CONTENTS

Introduction		3
Verbs		
1	Talking about the Present: Present Simple v. Present Continuous	4
2	Talking about the Past: Past Simple v. Past Continuous	5
3	Relating Past & Present: Past Simple v. Present Perfect	6
4	Present Perfect Continuous	8
5	Present Perfect v. Present Perfect Continuous	10
6	The Past Perfect	12
7	Talking about the Future: various forms	14
8	The Future in the Past	16
9	The Future Perfect	18
10	Obligation and Prohibition:	20
11	Necessity and Exemption	22
12	Ability	24
13	Possibility	26
14	Probability and Certainty	28
15	Requests and Permission	30
16	*used to* and *would*	32
Revision test 1		33
17	The Third Conditional	34
18	Conditional: Expressing Possibility 1	36
19	Conditional: Expressing Possibility 2	38
20	Conditional: Expressing the Impossible or Unreal	40
21	*unless* v. *if not*	42
22	Wishing	44
23	Reported Speech: Statements	46
24	Reported Speech: Questions, Orders and Requests	48
25	Gerund v. Infinitive 1	50
26	Gerund v. Infinitive 2	52
27	Preferences	54
28	The Passive	56
Revision Test 2		57
Determiners		
29	Articles	58
30	*much/many; very/to*	60
31	*few/little* v. *a few/a little*	62
32	Numbers	64
33	Possessives	66
Modification		
34	Adverbial and Prepositional Phrases: Position	68
35	Order of Adjectives	70
Revision test 3		71
Links		
36	Relative Clauses: Summary	72
37	Reduced Relative Clauses	74
38	Noun Clauses	76
39	Connectors: *nevertheless/however/therefore*	78
40	Conjunctions: Showing Reason	80
41	Conjunctions: Showing Result	82
Revision Test 4		83
Exit Test		84
Irregular Verbs		86
Punctuation and Spelling		87

Pearson Education Limited
Edingburgh Gate
Harlow
Essex CM20 2JE
England and associated companies throughout the world.

ISBN 0 582 42787 8

First published 2000
Copyright © Tim Kelly 2000

Designed by Mackerel
Printed in Scotland by Scotprint, Musselburgh

All rights reserved; no part of this publication may be reproduced, stored in a retrieval system, or transmitted in any form or by any means, electronic, mechanical, photocopying, recording or otherwise, without the prior written permission of the Publishers.

Published by Pearson Education Limited in association with Penguin Books Ltd, both companies being subsidiaries of Pearson plc.

Introduction

Penguin Grammar Workbook 3 is the third in a series of four workbooks. It is for students who have been learning English for a number of years and who are already familiar with the basic English grammatical structures. They may be preparing for exams such as the Cambridge First Certificate.

WHY IS GRAMMAR IMPORTANT?

Many people think that grammar is not important because people can understand them even when they make mistakes. People can understand simple information when you are telling them what you are doing or where you've been, even if you do make mistakes. When you want to talk about more complicated matters, mistakes can mean that the person you are talking to doesn't properly understand you. People might think they've understood you, but this is not certain. Correct grammar is important. It is like a key to the door of a language. Only when we use grammar correctly can we be sure that the listener has understood exactly what we wanted to say. For example, when we use the simple present, there is a different meaning to when we use the present continuous.

There is another reason why grammar is important. When you make mistakes, the listener has to be very careful about what you are saying. If you are always making mistakes, the other person will soon get tired of listening to you.

PENGUIN GRAMMAR WORKBOOK 3

The aim of this workbook is to provide students with a lot of practice work to improve the use of their grammar.

The workbook is divided into four sections:

UNITS 1 – 28: *Verbs*. Here there is practice for all the major English verb tenses, modal verbs like *can, must, may, should*, etc., conditional and passive forms and reported speech.

UNITS 29 – 33: *Determiners*. This section practises the use of the article, *the, a,* and *an*, words like *much, many, too, very, few* and *little*, numbers and possessives – *my, mine, his, hers* and so forth.

UNITS 34 – 35: *Modification*. Here there is work with adjectives, adverbs and prepositions.

UNITS 36 – 41: *Links*. In this section we look at ways of putting sentences together.

The 41 units in the book cover all the basic and many of the more complex English grammatical structures. In addition to practice with the way a structure is formed, there is also practice with how it is used.

A typical unit

1 Explanation Box Here you will find examples of the structure and short explanations of how it is formed and when it is used. Most of the boxes are in two parts: FORM and USE. In some cases, where the unit is comparing the use of two different structures, e.g. the Present Simple and the Present Continuous (Unit 1), we focus on the different uses of the two structures, showing how they are used to mean different things.

2 Practice Exercises Most of the units have five exercises. There is generally a progression from form-based to use-based exercises and from simpler to more difficult exercises.

Testing your grammar

At the end of each section there is a Revision Test. These are arranged in small groups. At the top of each group of items is an indication of which units they are testing, e.g. in Revision Test 1, you will see **UNITS 1 – 6** as one heading. This means the items in this group are testing the work in **Units 1 – 6**. In this way, you can see quickly what kinds of mistakes you are making and where you can find the information to help you get more practice.
At the end of the book, there is an Exit Test. Again the items are grouped according to the units they are testing. When you have done the Exit Test, you will see if you are ready to go on to Workbook 4.

The Answer Key

In the centre of the book, you will find the Answer Key for all the exercises and tests in this book. You can take this out of the book if you wish.

The End of the Book

At the end of the book there are three sections to help you:

1 Irregular verbs: this is a list of the most common irregular verbs, giving the infinitive, the simple past and the past participle.

2 Punctuation: this gives you information on when to use capital letters, commas and full stops.

3 Spelling: this is information to help you with plural and comparative forms.

FOR THE STUDENT

You can use this book to work on your own to improve your use of grammar. If you want to, you can work through the book from the beginning. We expect many of you, however, will want to spend more time practising the structures you find difficult. Different people will have different problems. Look at the contents page at the beginning of the book. This will tell you where you can find the grammatical structures you are looking for.

Always read the explanation box carefully before doing the practice exercises. It is not necessary to do every exercise at once. You may wish to do only one or two and go back to the others at a later date. This will give extra practice when you feel you need it.

Some of the exercises are in the form of dialogues (e.g. Unit 3, Exercise 2). On these occasions try to practise speaking the dialogue with a friend.

FOR THE TEACHER.

You can use this book as a grammar course book or as a supplementary book to give your students extra practice when they need it. It will be also useful for homework tasks.

In the classroom, the exercises which are marked with an asterisk (*), such as dialogues (e.g. Unit 3, Exercise 2) can be used for pair work and role play. There are also exercises marked with two asterisks (**) (e.g. Unit 15, Exercise 4) which can be used for discussion and group work tasks.

The answer key is in the centre and can be removed if you do not wish your students to use it when they are doing their homework.

Edward Woods and Tim Kelly

UNIT 1

Talking about the Present: Present Simple v. Present Continuous
Jack drinks coffee v. Jack is drinking coffee

USE

PRESENT SIMPLE
We use the present simple
1 to talk about states in the present which last a long time:
*Paula **lives** in Leeds.*
2 to talk about habits or things that happen regularly:
*I **read** a newspaper every day.*
3 to talk about states in the present at the moment of speaking:
*You **look** ill.*
4 to express general truths or facts
*The sun **rises** in the East and **sets** in the West.*
*Water **freezes** at 0°C.*

PRESENT CONTINUOUS
We use the present continuous
1 to talk about states in the present which are temporary:
*Paula **is living** in Leeds at the moment.*
2 to talk about activities or processes:
*You **are reading** this book.*

Note:
Because some verbs suggest a state rather than a process or activity they are not often used in the continuous form. We call them state verbs.
Some of the more common examples are *be, believe, belong, cost, presume, forget, realise, have* (meaning possess) *(I have a bicycle)* or *suffer from (I have a headache), remember, seem, hate, suppose, hear, think* (meaning believe), *know, understand, like, want, love*
At times, however, we use these verbs to express a process or activity and then we use the continuous form. Look at the statements:
*I **think** that money is more important than love.*
*I **am thinking** about my girlfriend.*
The first statemnet is an opinion (a general truth – in the speaker's mind). The second statement tells us what is going on in the speaker's mind at the moment – a process which will change as soon as the speaker begins thinking about something else.

1 Choose the correct sentence**

Choose the correct sentence (a or b). In some cases both sentences could be correct.
Example:
  (a) I believe him. ✓
  (b) I am believing him. ✗

1 (a) I think she is beautiful.
   (b) I am thinking she is beautiful.
2 (a) I think about the problem right now.
   (b) I am thinking about the problem right now.
3 (a) What does John look like?
   (b) What is John looking like?
4 (a) Does he look for something?
   (b) Is he looking for something?
5 (a) Andrew stays in Paris at the moment.
   (b) Andrew is staying in Paris at the moment.
6 (a) As sure as winter follows autumn, she will come.
   (b) As sure as winter is following autumn, she will come.
7 (a) It costs five dollars.
   (b) It is costing five dollars.
8 (a) Waiter! This food tastes awful!
   (b) Waiter! This food is tasting awful!
9 (a) Caroline's not in. She has a haircut.
   (b) Caroline's not in. She's having a haircut.
10 (a) I prefer tea to coffee.
   (b) I am preferring tea to coffee.
11 (a) She is doing the washing up every day.
   (b) She does the washing up every day.
12 (a) Who? I don't remember him.
   (b) Who? I am not remembering him.
13 (a) I am knowing that.
   (b) I know that.
14 (a) I can't stand her!
   (b) I can't be standing her!
15 (a) Catherine has a baby.
   (b) Catherine is having a baby.

2 Choose the use**

Look at your answers to Exercise 1 and choose the use each correct answer shows. Write the number of the sentence in the table. If there are two correct answers write (a) or (b) next to the number. The first one has been done for you.

PRESENT STATE: LONG TERM	
PRESENT STATE: TEMPORARY	
PRESENT STATE: MOMENT OF SPEAKING (STATE VERBS)	
ACTIVITY IN PROGRESS / TEMPORARY PROCESS	
HABIT / REGULAR HAPPENINGS	
FACT / GENERAL TRUTH	*1*

4

UNIT 2

Talking about the Past: Past Simple v. Past Continuous
They played football v. They were playing football

USE

PAST SIMPLE
We use the past simple
1 to talk about a finished event in the past:
*The train **left** the station.*
2 to talk about a finished action in the past:
*Yesterday, I **painted** the ceiling.*
This suggests the painting of the ceiling is finished.
3 to describe the main action or series of actions in narratives:
*Marlowe **stood** up, **took** a breath, and suddenly **felt** sick.*
4 to interrupt ongoing actions in the past:
*I **arrived** while/when they were arguing.*
or
*They were arguing when I **arrived**.*

PAST CONTINUOUS
We use the past continuous
1 to talk about something which was happening before an action or event in the past and continued to happen after it:
*While I **was drinking** coffee, the train left the station.*
2 to talk about an action which may not be finished:
*Yesterday, I **was painting** the ceiling.*

Here, we do not know if the painting of the ceiling has been finished or not.
3 to provide the background in narratives:
*The sun **was shining** and the birds **were singing**, but Marlowe felt sick.*
4 to talk about interrupted actions in the past:
*I arrived while/when they **were arguing**.*
or
*They **were arguing** when I arrived.*
5 to talk about intentions which were not fulfilled:
*I **was meeting** her this morning but I telephoned and rearranged the appointment.*

NOTE:
1 Be careful if using *when*. Look at the following sentences:
*Simon **hid** when he heard the door open.*
*Simon **was hiding** when he heard the door open.*
In the first sentence, Simon heard the door open first and then hid. In the second, Simon hid first and then heard the door open.
2 Some verbs are not usually used in the continuous form. (See Unit 1)

Complete the story

Complete the story by putting the verbs into the past simple or past continuous. Sometimes either form may be possible. The first one has been done for you.

The sun (1) *was shining* (shine) and the birds (2) .... (sing) but Marlowe (3) .... (feel) sick. As he (4) .... (walk) towards the exit he (5) .... (stop) and (6) .... (take) a deep breath. 'Better take it easy', Marlowe (7) .... (think). He (8) .... (walk) out of the gate and onto the sidewalk. Traffic (9) .... (pour) down Main Street, buses (10) .... (pick up) and (11) .... (drop off) passengers, taxis (12) .... (speed) in and out and frustrated car drivers (13) .... (honk) their horns. Marlowe (14) .... (watch) the traffic lights turn from green to red and then (15) .... (stumble) across the road. Pedestrians (16) .... (look) at him and (17) .... (step) aside to avoid any contact. One woman (18) .... (seem) like she (19) .... (come) towards him, as if to help, but Marlowe (20) .... (stare) at her so hard that she (21) .... (change) her mind and (22) .... (turn) away. Marlowe finally (23) .... (manage) to reach the other side and (24) .... (climb) the hospital steps when a nurse (25) .... (rush) down to help him.
Marlowe (26) .... (hold) his stomach with his hands. He (27) .... (remove) his hands and (28) .... (open) them. They (29) .... (be) red: red with blood. 'Oh, my God!', (30) .... (gasp) the nurse. 'What has happened?' (31) .... (demand) the doctor, arriving on the scene. Marlowe (32) .... (say): 'I (33) .... (walk) through the park when this big guy (34) .... (shoot) me.' Then Marlowe finally (35) .... (fade) into unconsciousness.

5

UNIT 3 — Relating Past and Present: Past Simple v. Present Perfect

Jack fell down v. Jack has fallen down

USE

PAST SIMPLE
We use the past simple
1 to talk about events that happened at particular times in the past:
Leonardo Da Vinci **painted** the Mona Lisa **in 1504**.
Jill **caught** a cold **yesterday**.
Did you **go** fishing **last summer**?
2 to talk about situations or events which happened regularly in the past:
We **spent every summer** fishing in the lake.
3 with *for* to talk about finished situations or events in the past:
I **lived** in Greece **for** two years. (I no longer live there)
4 with the following 'past tense' adverbials: *ago, yesterday, in 1987, last year,* and *on 21st of July*:
I **went** to Turkey **four years ago**.

PRESENT PERFECT
We use the present perfect
1 to talk about the present (or future) effects or results of events that happened at unspecified times in the past:
Little Leo **has painted** a beautiful picture. Come and see.
Jill **has caught** a cold and so won't be coming to school this week.
2 to talk about situations which began in the past and are still continuing:
He **has spent** four hours fishing already. (and is still fishing)
3 with *for* or *since* when something is still happening:
I **have lived** in Greece **for** two years. (I still live in Greece)
I **have lived** in Greece **since** 1997. (I still live in Greece)
4 with the following adverbials and prepositions: *ever, already, yet, up to, so far*:
Have you **ever been** to Turkey?
Note:
The following adverbials and prepositions can be used with either tense: *for, today, this morning, this month, this year, recently, before, once, just, already, yet* and *never*. American English prefers the simple past, British English the present perfect, although the choice of tense may depend upon the focus of the speaker.

1 Complete the answers*

Complete the answers using the past simple or present perfect.

Example:
Have you been to Switzerland?
Yes, I ...**have**..... I ....**went**....there last year.

1 Have you seen the Pyramids of Egypt?
  Yes, I .... I .... them in 1985.
2 Have you finished your homework?
  No, I .... yet.
3 Has Sheila arrived?
  Yes, she .... this morning.
4 Have you prepared dinner?
  Yes, I ....
5 Have you ever flown an aeroplane?
  No, I .... But I .... a helicopter two years ago.
6 Has Sharon put on her make-up yet?
  Yes, she .... She .... it on a few minutes ago.
7 Have John and Sylvia sold their house?
  No, they .... it yet.
8 Has Andrew cleaned my car yet?
  No, he .... And he .... mine either!
9 Have you ever told a lie?
  Yes, I .... I .... one this afternoon.
10 Sorry I'm late. Have you discussed last month's sales figures?
  Yes, we .... And we .... this month's figures too.

2 Complete the dialogue*

Complete the dialogue by putting the verbs into the past simple or present perfect. The first one has been done for you.

Scott: (1) ...**Have**...... you ever ....**been**..... (go) to Australia?
Tim: Yes, I (2) .... (go) there last year. I (3) .... (have) a wonderful trip. How about you; (4) .... you .... be (go)?
Scott: I (5) .... (visit) it many times. I (6) .... (travel) all over the continent – from Sydney to Perth, from Queensland to Tasmania. And what places (7) .... you .... (see) when you (8) .... (go) there?
Tim: Not so many. I (9) .... (spend) a few

days in Sydney, then **(10)** .... (fly) up to Cairns. I **(11)** .... (swim) in the sea around the Great Barrier Reef. The fish **(12)** .... (be) beautiful and the coral stunning. **(13)** .... you ever ....

Scott: Yes, indeed. I **(14)** .... (go) deep sea diving in the Coral Sea in 1993. And what **(15)** .... you .... (think) of Queensland?

Tim: It **(16)** .... (be) like a zoo without cages. There **(17)** .... (be) deadly jellyfish in the sea and crocodiles in the river.

Scott: And crocodiles in the sea, too.

Tim: **(18)** .... you ever .... (sit) on the back of a crocodile?

Scott: What? No, I haven't. Have you?

Tim: Yes: on a crocodile farm in Queensland.

Scott: You're joking!

Tim: No, really, it's true.

Scott: **(19)** .... (be not) you frightened?

Tim: I **(20)** .... (be) terrified. I **(21)** .... never .... (be) so frightened in my whole life.

Scott: Why **(22)** .... you .... (do) it?

Tim: Well, the owner of the crocodile farm **(23)** .... (say) it **(24)** .... (be) safe. He **(25)** .... (show) me what to do and **(26)** .... (assure) me Sheila – that's what he **(27)** .... (call) the crocodile – 'Sheila' – **(28)** .... (be) friendly. He **(29)** .... (offer) to give me a free dinner if I **(30)** .... (agree).

Scott: You must be joking.

Tim: How long **(31)** .... you .... (know) me, Scott? **(32)** .... I ever .... (tell) you a lie?

Scott: No, but...

Tim: Well, I simply **(33)** .... (approach) the crocodile from behind and **(34)** .... (lower) myself onto its back.

Scott: You're crazy!

3 Choose the correct sentence**

Choose the correct sentence (a) or (b).
Example:
(a) I stayed in Pakistan four years ago.   ✓
(b) I have stayed in Pakistan four years ago.   ✗

1 **(a)** Where did you go last night?
   (b) Where have you been last night?
2 **(a)** Where did you go since last night?
   (b) Where have you been since last night?
3 **(a)** I didn't dance the tango yet.
   (b) I haven't danced the tango yet.
4   Has the film already started?
   (a) Yes, it began.
   (b) Yes, it has begun.
5 **(a)** Look at this mess! Didn't you wash up for the last week?
   (b) Look at this mess! Haven't you washed up for the last week?
6 **(a)** We rehearsed every week that summer.
   (b) We have rehearsed every week that summer.
7 **(a)** What a beautiful house! Did you live here long?
   (b) What a beautiful house! Have you lived here long?
8 **(a)** I am a vegetarian. I didn't eat meat for five years.
   (b) I am a vegetarian. I haven't eaten meat for five years.
9 **(a)** I exercised every day but I don't any more.
   (b) I have exercised every day but I don't any more.
10 **(a)** Human beings existed on Earth for less than 10 million years.
   (b) Human beings have existed on Earth for less than ten million years.
11 **(a)** Dinosaurs existed on Earth for about 150 million years.
   (b) Dinosaurs have existed on Earth for about 150 million years.
12 **(a)** I didn't speak French until I was twenty.
   (b) I haven't spoken French until I was twenty.

4 Choose the use**

Look at your answers to Exercise 3 and choose the use each one shows. Write the number of the sentence in the table. The first one has been done for you.

UNFINISHED PAST EVENT	*1*
PAST (FINISHED) EVENT	
REGULARLY OCCURRING PAST EVENTS	
PAST (FINISHED) EVENT + FOR	
PAST EVENT + PAST ADVERBIAL	
PRESENT EFFECT OF PAST EVENTS	
UNFINISHED EVENT + FOR /SINCE	
PAST EVENT + PERFECT ADVERBIAL	

UNIT 4   The Present Perfect Continuous

FORM

Look at these sentences:
*I **have been** sleeping.*
*She **has been** working.*
The present perfect continuous has three parts:
have/has + *been* + present participle (the *-ing* form)
We usually shorten the form in spoken English:
*I've **been** sleeping.*
*She's **been** working.*
THE NEGATIVE
To form the negative we add *not* after *have* or *has*:
*I **have not been** sleeping.*
*She **has not been** working.*
In spoken English we usually shorten this by adding *n't* to *have* or *has*:

*I **haven't been** sleeping.*
*She **hasn't been** working.*
We can also shorten this by adding '*ve* or '*s* to the subject, though this is less common (and usually emphasizes the negative):
*I've **not been** sleeping.*
*She's **not been** working.*
THE QUESTION FORM
To form questions we put *have* or *has* in front of the subject:
*Have you **been** sleeping?*
*Has she **been** working?*

USE

1 We use the present perfect continuous to express
A continuous actions started in the past and just finished:
   *I've **been baking** a cake.*
B continuous actions started in the past and continuing into the present:
   *We've **been staying** at this hotel all week.*
C repeated actions or events started in the past and continuing into the present:
   *We've **been staying** at the same hotel every summer for the past ten years.*
2 The present perfect continuous is normally used with *for* and *since*. *For* is used to express duration (a length of time):

*They **have been travelling** round Africa **for two months**.*
*She **has been growing** vegetables **for many years**.*
Since is used to express a period of time, starting at a definite point in the past, and extending to the present:
*We **have been selling** newspapers **since 1985**.*
*He **has been asking** her to marry him ever **since he returned**.*
Note
1 Some verbs are not normally used in the continuous form. (See Unit 1.)
Note
2 The present perfect continuous takes the same adverbials as the present perfect – it is not used with 'past tense' adverbials.
(See Unit 3)

1 Complete the sentences

The following people are tired. Why? Complete the sentences with the present perfect continuous to find out.
Example:
Christy <u>has been playing</u> football.

1 Joyce .... (do) the washing.
2 Andrew and Chris .... (clean) the car.
3 Michael .... (cook) the dinner.
4 Joseph and Daniel .... (swim).
5 I .... (work) all day.
6 Catherine and Hugh .... (dance) the tango.
7 You .... (study) hard.
8 Martin .... (staying up late) every night.
9 We .... (decorate) the living room.
10 The actors .... (give) an exhausting performance.
11 Hannah .... (climb) a mountain.
12 The porter carry .... (bags) all day long.

2 Complete the interview*

Complete the interview with the musician by making questions for the answers.
Example:
Interviewer: How long <u>have you been playing the piano?</u>
Musician I've been playing the piano since I was three.

Int: How long **(1)** .... on this tour?
Mus: I've been travelling for about six months.

Int: Do you practise every day? **(2)** .... today?
Mus: Yes, for about four hours.
Int: There are many things to do in our city. What else **(3)** .... since you arrived here?
Mus: I've been visiting the sights, eating wonderful food and relaxing.
Int: Do you listen to other pianists? For example, **(4)** .... any today?
Mus: No, I rarely listen to other performers.
Int: I know you like reading. **(5)** .... anything interesting here?
Mus: Yes, I've been reading a new book about Mozart.

3 Right or wrong**

Put a tick ✓ or cross ✗ beside each sentence.
Example
We've been sailing in our yacht four years ago. ✗
They have been listening to music for hours. ✓

1 I've been trying to pass my driving test for five years.
2 The satellite has been orbiting the Earth last year.
3 They have been using the Channel Tunnel since 1995.
4 They have been building this road two years ago.
5 The secretary's been typing letters all afternoon.
6 My brother's been working for the GEC in 1989.
7 Dr Neutron led the project since it began.
8 They've been celebrating their exam success all night.
9 I've been working on this exercise at nine o'clock.
10 How long have you been knitting that jumper?
11 What have you been doing the month before last?
12 I haven't been doing anything.

4 Complete the sentences

Complete the sentences by putting the verbs in the past simple or present perfect continuous.
Examples:
I *have been thinking* (think) about what you said since yesterday.
The neighbours ..*didn't like*... (not like) us when we first moved in.

1 We .... (have) an automatic car for two years.
2 I .... (consider) the offer and will let you know my decision shortly.
3 Before there were cars and buses, people .... (travel) by horse and carriage.
4 He .... (be) a good boy.
5 I .... (not have) a good time, recently.
6 I .... (mean) to tell you for ages.
7 We .... (appear) on stage together for five years before I left.
8 We .... (appear) on stage together for five years and I suppose we will continue to appear together for five more.
9 I .... (not remember) to post that letter.
10 We're happy because we .... (remember) the past.
11 I .... (go) there for the last three years.
11 I .... (go) there three years ago.

5 Fill in the gaps*/**

Re-arrange the letters to make words and use them to fill in the gaps.

GTIWIRN	AINTWGI	GPIRODCUN
MGNIOC	LTAGNRLVEI	GNATIKL
IIDNTGENN	NRIGAIN	RGIRPEPAN
OGNRIGNI	DEWINGRAN	BNTAREELCGI

Example:
KOGIOLN
I've been ..*looking*.... for my pen for ages.

1 This factory's been .... cars or fifty years.
2 We've been .... for the party since Monday.
3 The lecturer has been .... for an hour and all the students are sleepy.
4 We've been .... to London for our holidays for the last three years.
5 I've been .... to clear that cupboard for months.
6 She's been .... letters since lunchtime.
7 How long have you been .... for your exam results?
8 The team have been .... their victory all night.
9 It's been .... all day and I'm wet all over.
10 They've been .... round Britain for two weeks.
11 You've been .... me. Are you angry with me?
12 I have been .... round the shops.

UNIT 5 Present Perfect v. Present Perfect Continuous

USE

Both the present perfect and the present perfect continuous refer to past events that usually extend until now (or beyond).

PRESENT PERFECT
When we use the present perfect
1 the period of time can be short or long without a time adverbial:
*Rice consumption in Japan **has fallen** rapidly.*
Here, the time that is referred to could be short if we add *recently* or *this summer*, or long if we add *over the last twenty years*.
2 the focus is on the present result of a past activity.
*Brendan **has baked** a cake.*
In this example we are interested in the result of Brendan's past activity (the cake) rather than the activity (baking). Therefore the following sentence is very unusual:
*Brendan **has baked**. (x)*

PRESENT PERFECT CONTINUOUS
Unlike the present perfect, the present perfect continuous usually focuses on the activity. This suggests the activity started recently unless a time adverbial says otherwise:
1 *Rice consumption in Japan **has been falling** rapidly.*
In this example we assume the fall of rice consumption began fairly recently.

2 the focus is on the activity rather than the result:
*Brendan **has been baking** a cake.*
Here, we are perhaps more interested in the activity (Brendan has been busy and so couldn't go shopping etc.,) than in the result. Therefore, the following sentence is quite acceptable:
*Brendan **has been baking**.*
As the present perfect continuous emphasizes activity rather than result, the result (the cake) need not be mentioned.

PRESENT PERFECT and PRESENT PERFECT CONTINUOUS
Sometimes, both the present perfect and present perfect continuous can be used. With verbs such as *live, sleep, study, work,* which describe activities that continue over a time period, both tenses are correct:
*I **have studied** English for seven years.*
*I **have been studying** English for seven years.*

Note:
Do not confuse the present perfect continuous with the passive form of the present perfect. Note the following forms:
*She **has done** it.*   present perfect
*She **has been doing** it.*   present perfect continuous
*It **has been done** (by her).*   present perfect passive

1 Describe the trends

The table below shows sales figures for various consumer goods. Look at the information in the table and complete the sentences using the words in the box. Use either the present perfect or present perfect continuous. In some cases both tenses are possible.

	1960	1970	1980	1990	2000
Cars	21,000	21,500	22,000	22,500	............?
Computers	0	0	2,000	5,000	............?
Black & White TVs	50,000	55,000	20,000	2,000	............?
Videos	0	1,500	10,000	15,000	............?
Fridges	15,000	15,030	15,000	15,025	............?
Bicycles	10,000	9,500	9,000	8,500	............?

Increase	rapidly
Decrease	steadily
Remain Steady	slightly

Example:
Sales of cars have increased steadily.
1 Sales of computers ....
2 Sales of black and white televisions ....
3 Sales of videos ....
4 Sales of fridges ....
5 Sales of bicycles ....

2 Complete the sentences

Complete the sentences by putting the verb into the present perfect or present perfect continuous.
Example:
*I **have been cooking** (cook)*

1 I have a sore throat because I .... (shout).
2 They .... (run) four kilometres to reach us.
3 Up to the present point in her career, she .... (write) twenty-five books.

4 Oh no! Look what you .... (do)!
5 You .... (break) my beautiful vase!
6 Hello! How are you! What .... (do) lately?
7 I .... (write) my latest novel. I .... (reach) the mid-point.
8 .... you ever .... (read) Tolstoy's *War and Peace*?
9 He .... (stare) out to sea for hours.
10 You .... (answer) my question.

3 Find the tenses**

In 1997 an environmental disaster happened in South-East Asia. Find the verbs in the present perfect and present perfect continuous in this newspaper report and underline them. (There are eight.) The first one has been done for you.

A dense cloud of smoke <u>has descended</u> over parts of South-East Asia. The smoke has led to a fall in daytime visibility which now is as little as five metres. People have been wearing masks to aid breathing. The vulnerable – especially the very old and very young – have been suffering the awful consequences of the smoke on their health. Patients have been waiting outside hospitals unable to cope with the growing numbers of the sick and dying. The Indonesian Government has declared a state of national emergency and has told people to stay indoors.

Environmental and wildlife protection groups have declared this the greatest environmental catastrophe for decades and warn that the repercussions are not simply national but international as the smoke gradually spreads its way across South-East Asia and the globe.

4 Complete the table

Complete the table by writing all the underlined verbs from Exercise 3 in the correct place. Where possible fill in the empty space in the column next to the verb with the appropriate verb form. One has been done for you.

PRESENT PERFECT	PRESENT PERFECT CONTINUOUS
has descended	(has been descending)

5 Complete the dialogue*

Complete the dialogue by putting the verbs into the present perfect or present perfect continuous. If both tenses are possible, write both. The first one has been done for you.

Mike: Hello darling, I'm home. You look hot. What **(1)** you ..**have**.. you **been doing**.? (do) **(2)** .... you .... ? (jog)
Heather: No, I haven't. I **(3)** .... (cook).
Mike: Oh, but why are you so hot?
Heather: Because I **(4)** .... (work) in a hot kitchen.
Mike: Oh, I see. **(5)** .... you .... (finish) yet?
Heather: No, not yet. I **(6)** .... (prepare) the soup, and **(7)** .... (put) the meat in the oven, but I **(8)** .... (not make) the pudding yet.
Mike: How long **(9)** .... the meat .... (cook)?
Heather: It **(10)** .... (roast) for two hours but it's not ready yet. Are you hungry?
Mike: Yes. I **(11)** .... (have) a hard day at work. One of the office computers broke down and I **(12)** .... (try) to get it going since late morning. I didn't stop for lunch and **(13)** .... (not eat) all day. It's a shame the meat isn't ready. I **(14)** .... (dream) about something hot and juicy all afternoon.
Heather: Oh, never mind dear. I have something hot and creamy for you. The soup is ready. It **(15)** .... (boil) for long enough. Let's eat!
Mike: Let's eat!

UNIT 6 The Past Perfect

FORM

Look at these sentences:
I **had been** to Egypt twice before I went in 1997.
At that time I **hadn't passed** my driving test, so Anne drove.
Had the Prime Minister already **decided** to change his party's policy when he made the announcement?

We make the past perfect as follows:
had + past participle
Had is often shortened to 'd:
I'd been to Egypt twice before I went in 1997.

USE

We use the past perfect
1 to talk about events or states which happened before a point of time in the past:
He sent me a card last week, even though he **had sent** one already.
2 to describe reccurring events in the past:
I **had seen** her every day last week.
Note:
The past perfect helps put events in a chronological (time-based) order. If two events occurred in the past then we can make clear which came first by using the past perfect and which came later by using the simple past.
Note how in the first four examples above the last event is written in the simple past and the event that came before it in the past perfect.
Look at the following table:

THEN: PAST SIMPLE (a point of time in the past)	BEFORE THEN : PAST PERFECT (a time before a point of time in the past)
I went to Egypt in 1997.	I had been to Egypt twice before. (before 1997)
Anne drove. (at that time)	I hadn't passed my test. (before and up to 'that time')
He made the announcement.	Had he already decided ? (at some time before he made the announcement)
He sent me a card last week.	He had sent one already. (before last week)

1 Match the parts

Match the parts in **A** with the ones in **B** to make statements about arriving too late.
The first one has been done for you.

A
1 The restaurant had closed
2 The ship had sunk
3 He had stopped breathing
4 The film had started
5 The deadline had expired
6 The children had gone
7 The supermarket had shut
8 The snow had melted
9 The sky had clouded over
10 The house had burnt down

B
(a) before the fire engine arrived.
(b) when she made her application.
(c) by the time she went shopping.
(d) when they lay down to sunbathe.
(e) when they reached the ski-slope.
(f) by the time we entered the cinema.
(g) when the rescue boats got there.
(h) before the diners arrived.
(i) by the time the doctor arrived.
(j) when the teacher returned.

2 Write sentences

Write sentences from the information below. Write the event that happened first in the past perfect and the event that followed in the past simple. Use the person or pronoun in brackets shown.

Example:
go walk / stop raining (I)
After it had stopped raining I went for a walk.

1 do the gardening / have a bath (he)
2 investigate the crime / arrest the criminal (the police)

3   become famous / write a novel (she)
4   do the washing-up / eat (he)
5   sell the car / take the bus (we)
6   count the money / make a collection (they)
7   go to bed / have a bath (the girl)
8   save enough money / buy a car (I)
9   the accident happen / the ambulance arrive
10 collect the wood / light a fire (the campers)

3 Complete the story

Complete the story by putting the verbs into the present perfect, past simple, past continuous or past perfect. If more than one tense is possible, write both. The first one has been done for you.

The police (1) **have captured** (capture) the famous jewel thief Craig, better known as 'Crafty' Craig. They (2) .... (arrest) him last night following a disturbance near to a night club in one of the seedier districts of the city of Sheffield. Dancers emerging from the night club (3) .... (hear) the sound of gunfire. One witness (4) .... (already hear) men arguing before a shot (5) .... (ring out). The police (6) .... (arrive) moments later. A local resident (7) .... (call) them on hearing the shot. Craig (8) .... (shoot) his partner in crime, the notorious gangster 'Mad Dog' McRae, who was left dying in a pool of blood. The two criminals (9) .... (fall out) over gambling debts and protection payments. Apparently Mad-Dog McRae (10) .... (attempt) to shoot Craig when 'Crafty' (11) .... (turn) the gun on its owner. The police (12) .... (catch) Craig as he (13) .... (try) to break into a nearby car to make his escape. Police (14) .... (discover) a diamond in Craig's pocket worth ten million pounds. Craig (15) .... (steal) the diamond from a warehouse belonging to the Greek movie tycoon, Yiannis Koufonikos, only days before.
   The police officer in charge of the operation, Detective Inspector Rowley Poley, (16) .... (issue) the following statement earlier today: We are very pleased to (17) .... (solve) the mystery of the missing diamond and to (18) .... (catch) Crafty Craig. Although all deaths are regrettable, Mad Dog McRae will not be missed by any decent citizens, nor others for that matter, as he was killed by one of his own kind. It could be said that Craig (19) .... (do) the world a favour by this act. In all my years of experience, I (20) .... (never know) a more sordid, evil and degenerate pair of criminals than Crafty Craig and 'Mad Dog' – or more exactly 'Dead Dog' McRae.

4 Fill in the table

Write down all the verbs you underlined in Exercise 3 in the table.

PAST PERFECT	PRESENT PERFECT	PAST SIMPLE	PAST CONTINUOUS

UNIT 7   Talking about the Future: various forms

FORMS

There are many ways of talking about the future. Here are the main forms.
present simple
The plane **departs** at 7.30 p.m.
present continuous
What **are you doing** tonight?
will (or shall) + infinitive
She'**ll be** 18 next month.
Shall I **help**?

will (or shall) + be + -ing
I'll be working at home next week.
going to + infinitive
I'm **going to buy** a car next month.
be about to + infinitive
The film **is about to start.**
be to + infinitive
All personnel **are to report** to security before leaving.

USE

PRESENT SIMPLE
We use the present simple for future events which are already fixed now such as in timetables and planned dates. This is a more formal use.
The train **arrives** at 11.00 a.m.
PRESENT CONTINUOUS
We use the present continuous for arrangements which exist now for the future. This is a common use.
What **are you doing** next week?
I'**m going** on holiday.
WILL (or SHALL) + INFINITIVE
1   We use will (or shall) + infinitive for predictions:
It **will rain** soon.
2   for promises, offers and requests
Will you **come** with me?
Yes, I **will** (come with you). And I'**ll carry** the bag.
3   for decisions made at the moment of speaking
Do you think I should accept the offer?
Yes, I do.
All right, I **will** (accept the offer).
4   for suggestions (Shall):
Shall we **have** a party on Saturday?
WILL (or SHALL) + BE + -ING
1   We use will (or shall) + be + -ing for predictions (emphasizing an activity):

More than 500 million people **will be watching** the World Cup final tomorrow.
2   to make polite enquiries (and indirect requests):
Will you **be using** the computer this evening?
No I **won't**. Do you want to use it?
Yes, if you don't mind.
GOING TO + INFINITIVE
We use going to + infinitive for predictions based on evidence, and for intentions:
It's **going to stop raining.**
I'm **going to accept** the offer.
BE ABOUT TO + INFINITIVE
We use be about to + infinitive to talk about the very near future:
  The opera **is about to** begin.
BE TO + INFINITIVE
We use be to + infinitive to refer to a future plan or programme. This is a formal use, found mostly in written English:
The President **is to make** a policy statement later today.
All foot passengers **are to proceed** to Deck C for disembarkation.
Note:
Shall is now not used a lot, except in suggestions.

1 Complete the sentences

Complete the sentences about the future by putting the verbs in either the present or present continuous.
Example
  ....*Are*...... you ....*meeting*.. (meet) Isabel this afternoon?

1   I .... (have) lunch with Karen tomorrow.
2   When .... the restaurant ....? (close)
3   .... he .... (see) her tonight?
4   I .... (take) Granny to the hospital at three o'clock.
5   His flight .... (take) four hours.
6   The tour .... (begin) at 2 o'clock.

2 Complete the sentences

Complete the sentences using be to + *infinitive or* be about to + *infinitive.*
Examples:
Hurry up. The show ..*is about to begin*.. (begin).
They ..*are to be married*.. (marry) on Friday.

1 The Pope .... (visit) Ireland in July.
2 I can only spare a minute as I .... (leave).
3 The crowd is restless. The players .... (enter) the stadium.
4 Just be patient. I .... (do) it.
5 The Director .... (announce) his retirement later today.
6 Representatives of the two countries .... (meet) this afternoon.

3 Match the sentences

Match the sentences in A with the ones in B. The first one has been done for you.

A
1 Look at the dark skies.
2 Will you do my homework for me?
3 There's a musical on tomorrow.
4 What time will you arrive?
5 It's hot in Spain.
6 I decided last night about the house.
7 What will you do now you've lost your job?
8 My legs are weak.
9 What are you doing this summer?
10 What are you doing this summer?

B
(a) Shall we go?
(b) Will you help me upstairs?
(c) I'm going to buy it.
(d) It's going to rain.
(e) No I won't. Do it yourself.
(f) I'm going to drive around Scotland.
(g) I'm not sure. Maybe I'll drive around Scotland.
(h) I'll be there about 2.00.
(i) I'll go home and start looking for a new one.
(j) You'll get sunburnt.

4 Choose the use**

Look at your answers to Exercise 3 and choose the use each pair of sentences shows. Write the number of the pair of sentences in the table. The first one has been done for you.

PREDICTION	
PREDICTION WITH EVIDENCE	*1*
REQUEST	
SUGGESTION	
DECISION MADE AT THE MOMENT OF SPEAKING	
DECISION MADE BEFORE SPEAKING	

5 Complete the dialogues*

Complete the dialogues using will + be + -ing.
Example:
Martin: ....*Will*...... you.. *be meeting* (meet) Jackie later?
Hector: Yes, I will. Why?
Martin: Could you ask her to give me a call.

1 **Hector:** .... you .... (go) shopping this morning?
  Martin: Yes. Do you want something?
  Martin: : Could you bring me a tin of dog food.
2 **Martin:** .... you .... (drive) into town today?
  Hector: Yes. Do you want a lift?
  Martin: That would be great.
3 **Hector:** Who .... (supervise) my thesis?
  Martin: Professor Kelly.
  Hector: That's a relief. I thought it might be Dr. Woods.
4 **Hector:** Who .... (lead) the investigation?
  Martin: Inspector Lestrade.
  Hector: Oh, dear. We'd better call Sherlock.
5 **Martin:** .... you .... (stay) home this weekend?
  Hector: I don't think so. Why?
  Martin: Just curious.

UNIT 8 The Future in the Past

FORMS

There are a number of ways of talking about the future from the point of view of a time in the past. Here are the most common forms:
1 was/were + going to + infinitive
I **was going to** write.
They **were going to** leave.

2 was/were + about to + infinitive
She **was about to** leave when I entered the room.
3 past continuous
They **were holding** the carnival the following week.

USE

We use
1 was/were + going to + infinitive to talk about plans or intentions that were not fulfilled. In I was going to write, the speaker did not fulfil his or her intention to not write and could be expanded as follows:
I **was going to write** but I didn't have a pen.
or
I **was going to write** but I couldn't be bothered.
or
I **was going to write** yesterday, but I was too busy, so I'll write today.
2 was/were + about to + infinitive to talk about intended actions which were interrupted the moment before they began (or at some stage before they were completed).
She **was about to leave** when I entered the room suggests that the woman (she) did not leave the room and might be found in the following situation:
I was late for the meeting. She had been sitting alone for half an hour and was getting annoyed. She finished her drink and went to pay the bill. She **was about to** leave when I entered the room. I apologized and bought her another drink. We sat down together and began talking. Her anger soon disappeared.
Even if the intended action is completed it is somehow interrupted or delayed:
She **was about to leave** when I entered the room. I apologised and begged her to stay but she would not listen. She walked angrily out of the door.
3 the past continuous to talk about an arrangement or plan made in the past for the future (from the point of view of that past time.) They **were holding** the carnival the following week suggests that at some time in the past they planned to hold a carnival for a later time (the following week) and we assume the carnival did take place unless told differently.
Note:
If, however, the was/were is stressed by the speaker this shows that the plan was not fulfilled.
They <u>were</u> holding the carnival the following week.
This suggests the carnival did not take place (or did not take place at the expected time) and might be expanded as follows:
They <u>were</u> holding the carnival the following week, but the weather became bad and they had to cancel it.
In written English stress is shown by <u>underlining</u> the word or writing it in italics.

1 Write sentences

Write sentences about the immediate future in the past using was/were about to + infintive.
Examples:
I / have a bath / the phone ring
I was about to have a bath when the phone rang.
The prisoners / the guard appear / escape
The prisoners were about to escape when the guard appeared.
1 She / close the shop / a customer enter
2 The pilot / the emergency light come on / take off
3 James / go out / Paul call round
4 He / the door open / knock
5 I / take the dog for a walk / it start raining

2 Did it happen?*

Read the following pairs (a) and (b) aloud, stressing any words in italics. Match these to the clauses (c and d) as appropriate. You can do this with a friend if you like.
Example:
(a) The horse was racing the next day
(b) The horse *was* racing the next day
(c) so the trainer let it rest after exercise.
(d) but it fell sick.
Answer: (a) matches (c) and (b) matches (d).

1 (a) They were going on holiday to Spain.
   (b) They *were* going on holiday to Spain.
   (c) but Yiannis invited them to Greece.
   (d) and had made careful preparations.
2 (a) He was giving up his job at the end of the month.
   (b) He *was* giving up his job at the end of the month.

(c) and then the manager offered him a salary increase.
   (d) and was starting a new one.
3 (a) She was meeting me later.
   (b) She *was* meeting me later.
   (c) by the river.
   (d) but she called and cancelled.
4 (a) He was having a birthday party at home on Friday.
   (b) He *was* having a birthday party at home on Friday.
   (c) and everyone was invited.
   (d) but decided to go out instead.
5 (a) We were playing in Liverpool next week.
   (b) We *were* playing in Liverpool next week.
   (c) and had to practise hard.
   (d) but the match has been postponed.
6 (a) She was singing in Milan in April.
   (b) She *was* singing in Milan in April.
   (c) but she caught a cold and lost her voice.
   (d) and was looking forward to it eagerly.

3 Match the parts

Match the parts in A and B to make sentences expressing what was going to happen but never did. The first one has been done for you.

A
1 Eddie was about to cut the grass
2 Brendan was going to be a doctor
3 Dennis *was* paying the bill
4 Eileen was about to walk home
5 Michelle was going to visit England
6 Sean was about to kick the ball
7 James *was* taking the photographs
8 Nancy was about to do the housework
9 Paddy *was* making dinner
10 Damien was going to marry a princess
11 Karen was going to be nice
12 Julie *was* doing the shopping

B
(a) when he tripped and hurt his leg.
(b) but she didn't save enough money for the flight.
(c) when the lawn mower broke down.
(d) but he forgot to buy film for his camera.
(e) when her friend offered her a lift.
(f) but he failed his medical exams.
(g) but he married a peasant instead.
(h) but his wife had already prepared it.
(i) when her relations arrived.
(j) but he had left his money at home.
(k) but by the time she was ready the supermarket was closed.
(l) but she couldn't help being rude and losing her temper.

4 Choose the use**

Look at your answers to Exercise 3 and choose the use each one shows. Write the number of the sentence in the table. The first one has been done for you.

UNFULFILLED INTENTION	
INTERRUPTED (INTENDED) ACTION	*1*
FUTURE PLAN (IN PAST) UNFULFILLED	

5 Write sentences

These famous people all intended to follow, or were expected to follow, a different career. Write a sentence about each person using going to do/be. *The first one has been done for you.*

	PERSON	INTENDED CAREER	ACTUAL CAREER
1	John Keats	surgeon	poet
2	Mahatma Gandhi	barrister	spiritual leader
3	Adolf Hitler	painter	politician
4	Sigmund Freud	scientist	psychoanalyst
5	H.G. Wells	zoologist	writer
6	Ludwig Wittgenstein	pilot	philosopher
7	James Joyce	priest	writer
8	Che Guevara	doctor	revolutionary
9	Joseph Stalin	monk	politician
10	Albert Einstein	violinist	physicist

1 John Keats **was going to** be a surgeon but he actually became a poet.

UNIT 9 The Future Perfect

FORM

Look at these sentences:
By the time you arrive, **I will have gone.**
We will have completed the report by the end of the week.
The future perfect has three parts:
will / shall / 'll + *have* + past participle

THE NEGATIVE
To form the negative add *not* after *will* or change *will* to *won't*:
She **will not have passed** her test by then.
I **won't have decided** until I've thought more about it.

THE QUESTION FORM
To form questions put *will* in front of the subject:
Will you have done it by Friday?

USE

We use the future perfect to say that an action will be completed or a state reached by a particular time in the future:
I **will have written** my novel by Christmas.
The restaurant **will have closed** by the time you get there.

It is commonly found after an *if* clause, to make a prediction:
If estimates are correct, the world's population **will have doubled** by 2020.
If I begin dieting now, I'll have lost weight in time for the summer holidays.

1 Write negative answers

Write negative answers to the following questions using the words in brackets.
Example:
Will you have made dinner by five o'clock? (six o'clock)
No, I won't have made dinner by five o'clock. I'll have made it by six o'clock.

1 Will your contract have expired by April? (May)
2 Will you have moved house by Christmas? (Easter)
3 Will you have bought a new car by summer? (winter)
4 Will you have paid me by this Friday? (next Friday)
5 Will I have received it by next week? (the week after next)
6 Will he have recovered before the holidays? (by the end of the holidays)
7 Will you have repaired it by this afternoon? (this evening)
8 Will the company have expanded by next year? (the year after next)
9 Will the rains have stopped by next week? (next month)
10 Will you have completed the project by 2010? (2020)
11 Will he have reached base camp by tomorrow? (the day after tomorrow)
12 Will you have done it by the time I arrive? (the time you leave)

2 Make forecasts

The table below shows the sales figures of a national book store and forecasts sales up to 2010. Look at the information in the table and write sentences about the estimated sales figures for 2010 using the words in the box.

| RISE TO + NUMBER / FALL TO + NUMBER / CEASE / NOT CHANGE |

BOOK TYPE	1980	1990	2000	2010*
Hardbacks	2,000	2,500	3,000	3,500*
Children's Books	4,000	5,000	5,500	6,500*
Novels	20,000	18,000	17,750	15,000*
Biographies	1,000	2,000	4,000	7,000*
School Books	2,000	2,000	2,000	2,000*
Academic Books	2,500	2,700	2,700	3,000*
Audio Books	0	100	1,000	3,000*
Factual Books	800	805	800	800*
Reference Books	400	380	350	300*
Special Interest Books	250	700	1,000	1,500*
Comics	700	200	50	0*
Magazines	1,000	3,000	7,000	10,000*
Newspapers	30,000	31,000	31,000	31,000*

* projected sales forecast (estimated)

Example:
Hardbacks
It is estimated that sales of hardbacks will have risen to 3,500 by 2010.
1 Children's Books
2 Novels
3 Biographies
4 School Books
5 Academic Books
6 Audio Books
7 Factual Books
8 Reference Books
9 Special Interest Books
10 Comics
11 Magazines
12 Newspapers

3 Complete the sentences

Make predictions by completing the sentences with the future perfect tense of the verbs in the box. The first one has been done for you.

> GO DISAPPEAR DECLINE MELT REPLACE SPEND STUDY WIDEN OVERTAKE CLOSE RISE DIE

1 Ten thousand French cafes *will have closed* by the end of the decade.
2 The number of deaths from disease .... by the end of the next decade due to improvements in medicine.
3 Over 90% of the world's population .... English by the end of the century.
4 The 'tiger' economies of the East .... the economies of the West in terms of economic power by the end of the century.
5 The divorce rate .... to over 50% by the end of the next decade.
6 The Amazonian Rain Forests .... by the end of the next decade if deforestation is not stopped.
7 At least one person from every country in the world .... to the moon by the end of the century.
8 The computer .... the human being as the central economic unit of production by the end of the century.
9 The polar ice-caps .... by the end of the century unless something is done to stop global warming.
10 The wealth gap between rich and poor .... by the end of the decade.
11 The Government .... 1000 million dollars on arms by the end of the year.
12 Ten million children .... from malnutrition and starvation in the Third World by the end of the century if there is not a significant redistribution of income from rich to poor.

4 Complete the dialogue **

Complete the dialogue below by putting the verb in brackets into the future perfect tense.

Dave: By the end of the summer, I (1) .... (earn) an extra £5,000.
Boris: What you (2) .... (do) to earn it?
Dave: Oh! I (3) .... (finish) making the furniture you want and I (4) .... (help) Terry install his sauna.
Boris: And during this time you (5) .... (continue) at the accountancy firm?
Dave: Of course. But I need more money than I get there. Mind you, by the end of August most of it (6) .... (go) repaying debts and things.
Boris: It (7) .... (pay) off all your debts?
Dave: For this year. But by next January, I (8) .... (receive) a fresh demand from the tax office and (9) .... (find) some other extra work.
Boris: Never mind. I (10) .... (think) of other things I need doing by then.
Dave: Thanks very much. But I hope I (11) .... (find) a better job than the one I have at the accountancy firm by then.

UNIT 10 Obligation and Prohibition: *must / mustn't / have to / have got to / should*

USE

OBLIGATION
We use
1 *must* to express obligation:
You **must** write your answers on the paper provided.
Silence **must** be observed during the examination.
This is formal usage and often used to state rules.
Have to is also *used to express obligation:*
You **have to** answer a hundred multiple choice questions.
This is less formal than **must**.
2 *should* to express a milder (i.e. avoidable) obligation:
You **should** read the instructions carefully before starting.
Should is not as strong as *must* and is often used to give advice:
You **should** dress smartly when going to your interview.
Note:
1 *Must* does not have a past form. We use the past of *have to* to express obligation in the past:
We **had to** be silent during the test.
Should have is used to express a past obligation, but an obligation which was not carried out – an unobserved obligation:
Julie **should have** telephoned last week.
This suggests that Julie did not in fact telephone last week.

2 *Must have* is not used for obligation in the past. It is used for past probability. (See Unit 14.)
PROHIBITION
We use *must not (mustn't)* to express prohibition:
Students **must not** eat in class.
Must not forbids action and so is often found in formal rules:
Passengers **must not** open the door until the train has stopped moving.
2 *Should not* (shouldn't) to express a milder (i.e. avoidable) prohibition:
You **shouldn't** talk while the teacher is talking.
Should not is often used to give advice or warnings:
You **shouldn't** wear those old clothes at your interview.
I **shouldn't** do that, if I were you.
Note:
The negative of *have to (don't have to)* does not mean the same as *mustn't*. If you don't have to do something, it is not necessary to do it, but you may do it if you wish. It has the same meaning as *needn't* and so expresses exemption. Compare the following sentences:
You **mustn't** say anything.
You **don't have** to say anything.
In the first example the subject *(you)* is not allowed to speak, whereas in the second example the subject may speak if he wishes, but does not need to. [See Unit 11.]

1 Write sentences

Write sentences about the swimming pool notice. Use must/mustn't or should/shouldn't to explain the rules, advice and warnings. You should write twelve sentences. The first one has been done for you.

ATTENTION SWIMMING POOL USERS
Please note that running, jumping, fighting and ducking are dangerous and are forbidden in the pool area. Avoid shouting as it can detract attention from a real emergency. We would advise those with serious health problems to consult their doctors before swimming. Allow at least half an hour after eating a large meal before swimming. Avoid swimming after drinking alcohol. If an emergency occurs please notify the attendant immediately. Do not attempt life saving unless you are qualified to do so. Children under 10 years old are not allowed to swim unless accompanied by an adult. The pool is a non-smoking area.
Thank you for your attention and please enjoy your swim.

1 *You mustn't run in the pool area.*

2 Choose the use**

Choose the use each sentence shows. Write the number of the sentence in the table. The first one has been done for you.

OBLIGATION	
MILD (AVOIDABLE) OBLIGATION	
PAST OBLIGATION	*1*
PAST (UNOBSERVED) OBLIGATION	
PROHIBITION	
MILD PROHIBITION	
EXEMPTION	

1 You had to wear a suit and tie for work when I was young.
2 You should write and thank people who send you birthday presents.
3 You must do your homework.
4 He has to leave tomorrow.

5   She shouldn't go out alone after dark.
6   We should have finished the job two days ago.
7   You don't have to go.
8   In the army you had to polish your boots until you could see your face in them.
9   You mustn't cry.
10 Factory employees must stamp their time cards on arrival.
11 Women have to wear a veil over their faces in some Muslim countries.
12 All people should have equal rights in a fair society.
13 Guests should vacate their rooms before 11 a.m. on their day of departure.
14 The treasurer must attend all meetings relating to finance.
15 The treasurer doesn't have to attend meetings on other matters.

3 Rewrite the sentences

Rewrite the sentences from Exercise 2 changing the past tenses into present tenses and present tenses into past where possible. Use time adverbials such as now, then *or* soon *to replace existing ones where a change of tense makes it necessary. If changes in meaning occur apart from time changes, then explain them. The first one has been done for you.*

1   *You have to wear a suit and tie for work now.* (no change)

4 Rewrite the questions

Rewrite the following questions as statements using should have *or* shouldn't have.
Examples:
Why haven't I been paid?
I should have been paid.
Why did you do it?
You shouldn't have done it.

1   Why were you late?
2   Why didn't they answer?
3   Why didn't you send the letter yesterday?
4   Why wasn't I told?
5   Why did you come?
6   Why have you forgotten your book?
7   Why did he lie?
8   Why weren't they happy?
9   Why has she behaved so foolishly?
10 Why did you believe him?
11 Why didn't you love her?
12 Why have the water-pipes cracked?

5 Fill in the table**

Fill in the table by putting the parts of sentences below into the best place to make full sentences. The first two have been done for you.

YOU MUSTN'T ...	YOU DON'T HAVE TO ...
tell lies	get up early at the weekends

1   tell lies
2   get up early at the weekends
3   finish the report tonight
4   forget your passport
5   be late
6   work late if you don't want to
7   talk in the library
8   finish your dinner
9   have coffee, I can make tea
10 smoke or you'll get cancer
11 throw stones
12 miss the appointment
13 invite her, though I'd like her to come
14 stay home, you can go out
16 Nobody must leave the building.
17 He doesn't have to work every weekend.
18 In Germany, you shouldn't cross the road when the red pedestrian light is against you.
19 You must have the correct fare when you travel on the 112 bus route. They don't give change.
20 I'm expecting a phone call, so I've got to be home by 8.30 this evening.

UNIT 11 Necessity and Exemption: *need to / needn't / don't need to / have to / have got to / don't have to / haven't got to*

USE

NECESSITY
1 We use *need to* to express necessity:
You **need to** take your medicine.
2 We also use *have to* to express necessity:
You **have to** take it after breakfast.
We can use *have got to* in informal English to express necessity:
You**'ve got to** go to the hospital.

EXEMPTION
1 We use *needn't* or *don't need to* to express exemption (to say it is not necessary to do something):
You **needn't** go immediately.
You **don't need to** go immediately.
These are alternative forms.
2 We also use *don't have to* to express exemption:
They **don't have to** send an ambulance.
We can use *haven't got to* in informal English:
You **haven't got to** see the doctor.

THE QUESTION FORM
1 To ask about necessity and exemption we use *Do (I) need to ...?* or *Need (I) ...?*

Do I **need** to take my medicine?
Need I take my medicine?
These are alternative forms.
1 We can also use *Do (I) have to ...?* or more informally *Have (I) got to ...?* to ask about necessity and exemption:
Do I have to go to hospital?
Have I got to go to hospital?
Note:
1 *Needn't, don't need to, don't have to* and *haven't got to* are often used in tag questions to request exemption:
I **needn't** go to hospital, need I?
I **don't need** to go to hospital, do I?
I **don't have to** go to hospital, do I?
I **haven't got to** go to hospital, have I?
2 *Need* is also a main verb:
I **need** my medicine.

1 Match the sentences

Match the sentences in **A** with the ones in **B**. The first one has been done for you.

A
1 My head aches.
2 The room is dirty.
3 The television isn't working.
4 My shoes aren't shiny.
5 The children are sleeping.
6 The weather's awful!
7 He's been sacked.
8 I can't come out yet.
9 He's getting fat.
10 I'm very tired.
11 She got poor results.
12 The boys are hungry.
13 I think I'm going crazy.

B
(a) I need to rest.
(b) We need to bring our coats.
(c) You need to clean it.
(d) He needs to diet.
(e) You need to take an aspirin.
(f) They need to eat.
(g) She needs to study harder.
(h) We need to get it fixed.
(i) I need to finish my homework.
(j) We need to be quiet.
(k) He needs to find a new job.
(L) I need to see a psychiatrist.
(M) You need to polish them.

2 Write the questions*

A child asks his parents if it is necessary to do certain things. The responses of the parents are written below. Write the child's questions to match the answers. Use *have to* or *have got to*.

Examples:
Child: .... *Have I got to go to school* ....?
Parent: Of course you have got to go to school.
Child: ...... *Do I have to do my homework* ......?
Parent: Of course you have to do your homework.

1 **Child:** ....?
   Parent: Of course you have to come with us.
2 **Child:** ....?
   Parent: Of course you have got to eat up all your dinner.
3 **Child:** ....?
   Parent: Of course you have got to tidy your room.
4 **Child:** ....?
   Parent: Of course you have to thank Auntie for her present.
5 **Child:** ....?
   Parent: Of course you have to comb your hair.
6 **Child:** ....?
   Parent: Of course you have got to take a bath.
7 **Child:** ....?
   Parent: Of course you have to brush your teeth.
8 **Child:** ....?
   Parent: Of course you have to put on your pyjamas.
9 **Child:** ....?
   Parent: Of course you have got to meet your cousin.
10 **Child:** ....?
   Parent: Of course you have to let him play with your toys.
11 **Child:** ....?
   Parent: Of course you have got to wash your hands.
12 **Child:** ....?
   Parent: Of course you have to help your sister.

---

3 Write sentences

Look at the information about two young people, Jackie and Arnold. Then write sentences about them. Use need to *or* needn't *with the help of the words in brackets. The first one has been done for you.*

	JACKIE	ARNOLD
1	weight – 50 kilos	weight – 100 kilos
2	height – 1.45 metres	height – 1.90 metres
3	hair – short	hair – long
4	healthy	unhealthy
5	introvert	extrovert
6	no friends	many friends
7	wears fashionable clothes	wears old scruffy clothes
8	short-sighted	normal vision
9	lazy	hard-working
10	has no illnesses	diabetic
11	School Test Score 44%	School Test Score 96%
12	father gives her money	has a part time job

1 *Arnold needs to diet, he weighs 100 kilos! (diet) Jackie needn't diet, she only weighs 50 kilos.*
2 (grow taller)
3 (get a hair cut)
4 (do more exercise)
5 (be more outgoing)
6 (be more sociable)
7 (dress more smartly)
8 (wear glasses
9 (work harder)
10 (take medicine)
11 (study more)
12 (work for money)

4 Choose the Use**

Choose the use each sentence shows. Write the number of the sentence in the table. (This exercise applies to both this and the previous unit.) The first one has been done for you.

1 We need to recruit two new members of staff.
2 All drivers must wear safety belts.
3 Should I come at nine o'clock?
4 You haven't got to listen to me any more, now you're leaving.
5 Do I need to come back?
6 He doesn't need to get a good grade: he's already been offered a job.
7 You mustn't worry.
8 I have to give a presentation tomorrow.
9 The chickens have got to lay one egg a day, or they are sold.
10 You don't have to answer immediately. Think about it first.

OBLIGATION	
AVOIDABLE OBLIGATION	
NECESSITY	*1*
EXEMPTION	
MILD PROHIBITION	
PROHIBITION	

UNIT 12 Ability: can / could / be able to

USE

We use
1 can to express ability in the present and future:
He **can** speak English.
I **can** come to the meeting tomorrow.
2 can't to express inability:
She **can't** juggle.
3 could to express ability in the past:
He **could** climb to the top of any tree in the forest.
I **could** swim across the lake when I was a young man.
4 couldn't to express inability in the past:
Most people **couldn't** read or write in the nineteenth century.
5 be able to to express ability in the past, present and future:
The prisoners **were able** to escape because they had stolen a key from the guard.
Martine the Magician i**s able** to hypnotize members of the audience.
I will **be able** to give you an answer next week.
6 be unable to and not be able to to express inability:
She **was unable** to swim the channel.
I **am not able to** fix the computer.
7 could have + past participle to express something that did not happen in the past, even though the ability to do it existed:
They **could have won** if they hadn't been unlucky.
We often use this form to show disapproval or as a reproach:
You **could have telephoned**!
8 couldn't have + past participle to suggest that someone did not have the ability to do something in the past:
He **couldn't have committed** the murder because he was sick in bed at the time.
They **could not have done** anything else.
There is not always a clear distinction between ability and possibility with this form. (See Unit 13.)

Note
1 Can and could are used more commonly than be able to.
2 Sometimes only be able to is possible. This is after to, with an -ing form or when using another modal verb:
1 I want **to be able to** play the clarinet.
2 The consequences of **being able to** explore outer space are only faintly imaginable.
4 You **may be able to** reach the top.

1 Fill in the gaps to match the parts

Fill in the gaps with can, can't, could or couldn't to match the parts in A with the parts on B. The first one has been done for you.

A
1   Would you mind sitting down?
2   I was stuck in customs for three hours.
3   I will come with you
4   She won the race!
5   Can you carry the bags upstairs?
6   I was asked to give a speech,
7   Please speak louder!
8   Try standing on my left.
9   When I was small
10 In our new factory
11 I wanted to believe him,
12 Don't be sad.

B
(a) I .... climb through the window.
(b) we .... produce twice the quantity at a lower price.
(c) I .... see over your head.
(d) I .... only hear in my left ear.
(e) but I .... after he'd lied to me.
(f) I .... be happy if you're not.
(g) I .... hear you!
(h) but I .... say a word.
(i) I .... believe it!
(j) if I ....
(k) because I .... find my passport.
(l) I .... carry the small bag, but I .... carry the big one: I'm not that strong.

2 Rewrite the questions as statements

Rewrite the following questions as statements using could have.
Example:
Why didn't you send me a letter?
You could have sent me a letter.

1. Why didn't you go to the concert?
2. Why didn't they ask me?
3. Why didn't she come?
4. Why didn't they tell you?
5. Why didn't Dennis bring his money?
6. Why didn't Wendy make a decision?
7. Why didn't the police arrest Purcell?
8. Why didn't Philip walk her home?
9. Why didn't they reduce the price?
10. Why didn't you buy me a present?
11. Why didn't he say he was innocent?
12. Why didn't you attend the interview?

3 Write responses

Write responses to your statements for Exercise 2 using couldn't have. *The reasons in the box will help you. You will have to choose from the following as they do not match the order of your answers to Exercise 2. The first one has been done for you.*

BECAUSE HE HAD TWISTED HIS ANKLE.

AS I HAD NO MONEY. SORRY!

BECAUSE I DIDN'T HAVE A TICKET.

UNTIL THEY HAD SEEN HIM COMMIT A THEFT.

BECAUSE THEY HAVEN'T SEEN ME FOR WEEKS.

BECAUSE SHE HAD ANOTHER ENGAGEMENT.

AS I GOT VERY NERVOUS, STARTED PANICKING, AND FAINTED.

BECAUSE ONLY THE MANAGER HAD THE AUTHORITY TO DO THAT.

UNTIL SHE WAS SURE OF ALL THE FACTS.

BECAUSE HE HAD LOST HIS WALLET, OR SO HE SAID.

BECAUSE THEY NEVER HAD A CHANCE TO SPEAK TO YOU.

BECAUSE HE WAS CAUGHT WITH THE STOLEN WATCH ON HIS WRIST.

1. *I **couldn't have gone** to the concert because I didn't have a ticket.*

4 Write sentences

George is an old man suffering from a terminal illness which affects the body and the mind. Look at the information in the table and write sentences about George using be able to *or* be unable to.

MEDICAL NOTES ON GEORGE SMITH		
5 YEARS AGO	NOW	IN 5 YEARS TIME
could walk and run normally	can walk 50 metres slowly	will need a wheelchair
could have a normal conversation	can speak but cannot understand other people	will only produce sounds, not words
could cook his own food	can't cook his own food, but can feed himself	will need to be fed
could wash himself	can wash himself, but needs help into the bath	will need washing

Example:
*Five years ago George was able to walk and run normally. Now George is able to walk fifty metres slowly. In five years time George **will be unable to walk**. He will need a wheelchair.*

5 Fill in the gaps**

Fill in the gaps where possible with can, can't, could *or* couldn't. *If it is not possible to use one of these then use* be able to, be unable to *or* be not able to.
Example:
I hope I ..... ***can*** ...... win the championship at some stage in the future.
I hope to .. ***be able to***.. win the championship at some stage in the future.

1. I was heartbroken at .... to see her again.
2. I was heartbroken because I .... see her again.
3. I think he's unconscious. It seems he .... hear me.
4. I think he's unconscious. He seems to .... hear me.
5. In the past most people .... afford a holiday.

UNIT 13 Possibility: *can / could / may / might*

USE

We use
1 *can* to express a general possibility:
*Skiing **can** be fun.*
2 *could* to express a specific possibility:
*Shall we go skiing next year? It **could** be fun.*
3 *can't* when something is not possible:
*It **can't** be true.*
*Theories about the origin of the universe **cannot** be proved.*
4 *may, may not, might* and *might not* to express a specific or general possibility:
*Skiing **may** be fun.* (general possibility)
*Skiing **might** be fun for some,*
*but it **might not** be for others.* (general possibility)
*Next year's ski trip **may** be fun,*
*but then again it **may not**.* (general possibility)
*I **might not** go.* (general possibility)
Note:
May, might and *could* express a less likely possibility than *can*. Compare the following sentences:
*You **can** get stamps from any post office.* (general possibility)
*You **may** get stamps from a corner shop.* (general possibility)
*You **might** get a stamp from the corner shop. I'm not sure.* (general possibility)
*You **could** get a stamp from the corner shop, if it were open.* (specific (im)possibility)

There is a progression from more likely to less likely in each of these sentences. The following table shows the different uses:

	SPECIFIC POSSIBILITY		
GENERAL POSSIBILITY			
CAN	MAY	MIGHT	COULD
MORE LIKELY ←			→ LESS LIKELY

5 *could have, may have, may not have, might have* and *might not have* + past participle to express a past possibility about which the speaker is uncertain:
*She **could have** seen me.*
*The shop **may have** been open.*
*She **may not have** killed her husband.*
*They **might have** told me already, I can't remember.*
*You **might not have** realized what was going on.*
6 *could have* to express a possibility in the past which did not occur:
*You **could have** told me the truth! (But you lied.)*
*The show **could have** been a disaster. (But it was a success.)*
5 *could not have* to express that it was not possible for something to happen in the past:
*I **couldn't have** made a mistake.*
*He **couldn't have** driven there as he doesn't have a car.*
(See also UNIT 12)

1 Fill in the gaps

Fill in the gaps with can *or* could *to express a general or specific possibility*
Example:
Mountain climbing ...*can*.... be dangerous.
Climbing Mount Everest next month ..*could*...be dangerous.

1 Going to the dentist ……… be painful.
2 Which dentist is going to treat you, Mr Russell? It ……… be painful.
3 If you continue to smoke twenty cigarettes a day you ……… get cancer.
4 Smoking ……… cause cancer.
5 Springtime in Scotland ……… be beautiful.
6 Next spring in Scotland ……… be wonderful.
7 Don't play the music so loud. You ……… damage our ears.
8 Playing music loud ……… damage your ears.
9 Wind surfing ……… be exciting.
10 This afternoon's wind surfing ……… be exciting.
11 Tomorrow's meeting ……… be boring.
12 Meetings ……… be boring.

2 Rewrite the sentences

Rewrite the sentences using may, may not, might *or* might not. *You can use either* may *or* might *as you like.*
Example:
She will probably go.
……*She might go*……
I don't think it's true.
……*It may not be true.*……

1 It's possible he'll get caught.
2 Perhaps the weather will improve.

3 She's uncertain if he will come.
4 Maybe my father will change his mind.
5 I'm not sure if the bank's open.
6 There is a chance you'll succeed.
7 It's possible he will die.
8 Perhaps it's broken.
9 I don't know if he's English.
10 I think it's his birthday this week. I'm not certain.
11 Do you think she'll agree to an interview? Possibly not.
12 Do you think he won't answer? I'm not sure.

3 Rewrite the sentences

Rewrite your answers to Exercise 2 in the past using may have, may not have, might have *or* might not have.

Example:
She might go.
She might have gone.
It may not be true.
It may not have been true.

---

4 Match the parts

Match the following sentences. The first one has been done for you.

1 It could have been Sheila.
2 It could have been a great party.
3 You could have caught the bus,
4 I could have picked it up by mistake
5 She could have had her hair dyed –
6 She could have changed her name.
7 You could have planned things better
8 We could have organised the event ourselves
9 The meeting could have ended an hour ago,
10 He could have lost his way.
11 He could have got the sales job last year.
12 We could have won the lottery.

(a) from blonde to red.
(b) Where could he be?
(c) But I think it was Sandra.
(d) It's a shame we let the council organize it.
(e) Let's check our numbers.
(f) Maybe she got married.
(g) Why did Dennis have to ruin it?
(h) But he wanted an office job.
(i) Why didn't you?
(j) if you missed the train.
(k) if the manager hadn't started talking.
(l) But I don't think I did.

---

5 Choose the uses**

Look at your answers to Exercise 4 and choose the use each one shows. Decide if the sentence is a possibility in the past about which the speaker is uncertain or a possibility in the past which the speaker knows did not happen. Write the number of the sentence in the table. Then state exactly what the speaker knows or is uncertain about. The first two have been done for you.

| SPEAKER UNCERTAIN | *1* |
| SPEAKER HAS KNOWLEDGE | *2* |

1 The speaker does not know if it was Sheila or if it was Sandra.
2 The speaker knows it was not a great party because Dennis ruined it.

6 Rewrite the sentences

Rewrite the sentences using couldn't have. *The words in brackets will help you.*

Example:
They never had any money. (be rich)
They couldn't have been rich.

1 He always made mistakes. (be clever)
2 She didn't understand me. (speak English)
3 He is a good swimmer. (drown)
4 They are poor. (buy a Rolls Royce)
5 I am always right. (make a mistake)
6 He has an awful voice. (join the choir)
7 Paul didn't bring his swimming costume. (go swimming)
8 I didn't write her a letter. (reply)
9 We told him. (be unaware)
10 Angela begged me. (refuse)
11 They were always arguing. (be friends)
12 He was on holiday. (help)

UNIT 14 Probability and Certainty: *ought / should / must / will / can't*

USE

OUGHT and SHOULD: PROBABILITY
We use
1 *ought* or *should* to express probability: to say that we think something will probably happen or is probably true:
*The room **ought** to be ready by next week.*
*I've fixed the television. It **should** work now.*
2 *ought not* or *should not* when we think something probably won't happen or probably isn't true:
*You **ought not** to get a poor picture on your television any longer.*
*It **shouldn't** cause you any more problems.*
3 *ought to have* + past participle or *should have* + past participle to express probability in the past:
*Their plane **ought to have landed** in Spain last night.*
*He **should have finished** work half an hour ago. He'll be home soon.*
We can also use these forms to express a probability in the past that didn't happen:
*Their plane **should have landed** in Spain last night, but it didn't arrive until this morning.*
4 *ought not to have* + past participle or *should not have* + past participle when we think something probably didn't happen in the past:
*They **oughtn't to have** found it difficult.*
*He **shouldn't have had** any problems at all.*
We can also use these forms to say that what happened in the past surprises us:
*They **oughtn't to have found** it difficult. Why did they?*

*He **shouldn't have had** any problems at all. I'm surprised he did.*

MUST and CAN'T: PROBABILITY – NEAR CERTAINTY
We use
1 *must* when we are almost certain something is true:
*You **must** be the new secretary. Hello.*
*He **must** think I don't know.*
2 *cannot* or *can't* when we are almost certain something is not true:
*She **can't** be in Rio. I saw her last night in London.*
*It **cannot** be true.*
3 *must have* + past participle to express near certainty in the past:
*We **must have taken** a wrong turning. We're lost.*
4 *can't have* + past participle when we think something did not happen in the past:
*We **can't have taken** a wrong turning as we've stayed on the same road all the way.*

WILL: CERTAINTY
We use
1 *will* to express certainty in the future:
You'll be sorry.
*It **will** arrive next week.*
2 *will not* or *won't* when something is certain not to happen in the future:
*You **will not** be granted a visa under present circumstances.*
*Don't try and escape. You **won't** make it.*

1 Write sentences

Andrew and Chris are going on a tour of Europe. Look at their plan and write sentences about their trip using should. *Write four sentences about what they are doing on the dates below. (You should write twenty sentences.)*

PLACE	ESTIMATED TIME OF ARRIVAL	DEPARTURE	DATE	TRANSPORT TO NEXT DESTINATION
Paris	Monday a.m.	Wednesday p.m.	1st–3rd	Aeroplane
Brussels	Wednesday p.m.	Friday a.m.	3rd–5th	Train
Amsterdam	Friday p.m.	Sunday a.m.	5th–7th	Train
Bonn	Sunday p.m.	Monday a.m.	7th–8th	Motor bikes
Munich	Monday p.m.	Thursday a.m.	8th–11th	Bus
Vienna	Thursday p.m.	Saturday p.m.	11th–13th	Night coach
Venice	Sunday a.m.	Thursday a.m.	14th–18th	Hire car
Milan	Thursday p.m.	Friday a.m.	18th–19th	Night train
Bern	Friday p.m.	Saturday p.m.	19th–20th	Aeroplane
Paris	Saturday p.m.	Sunday a.m.	20th–21st	Train
Calais	Sunday p.m.	Sunday p.m.	21st	Ferry
Dover	Sunday p.m.	Sunday p.m.	21st	Car
London	Sunday p.m.		21st	

Example:
Monday 1st – Wednesday 3rd
They should arrive in Paris on Monday morning.
They should leave Paris on Wednesday evening.
They should stay in Paris for two nights.
They should be on the aeroplane to Brussels on Wednesday evening.

1 Wednesday 3rd – Friday 5th
2 Friday 5th – Sunday 7th
3 Sunday 7th – Monday 8th
4 Monday 8th – Thursday 11th
5 Thursday 11th – Saturday 13th

2 Write sentences

Two friends are discussing what Andrew and Chris are doing while they are away. What do they say? Write sentences about the trip using ought to have. *Write four sentences about each of the specified dates. (You should write sixteen sentences.)*

Example:
Monday 1st – Wednesday 3rd
They ought to have arrived in Paris on Monday morning.
They ought to have left Paris on Wednesday evening.
They ought to have stayed in Paris for two nights.
They ought to have been on the aeroplane to Brussels on Wednesday evening.

1 Sunday 14th – Thursday 18th
2 Thursday 18th – Friday 19th
3 Friday 19th – Saturday 20th
4 Saturday 20th – Sunday 21st

3 Did it happen?**

Complete the sentences using should have *or* shouldn't have. *Then decide if the sentence describes a past happening which we assume has probably occurred (a), a past happening which we know did not occur (b), a past happening which probably hasn't occurred (c) or a past happening we know occurred (d).*

Example:
They ..**should have travelled**.. (travel) by bus as they don't have a car. (a)

He ..**should have been**.. (be) on stage five minutes ago. Where is he? (b)
They **shouldn't have travelled** (travel) by bus as they have a car. (c)
He ..**shouldn't have gone**.. (go) on stage until after the King and Queen had left. (d)

1 They …………. (go) out yet. Let's call. ( )
2 They …………. (go) out yet. It's a pity they have. ( )
3 She …………. (do) it. I'm very angry that she did. ( )
4 She …………. (do) it. Shall we ask, just in case she has. ( )
5 The news …………. (come) through by now. Let's telephone and find out. ( )
6 The news …………. (come) through by now. I wonder why it hasn't. ( )
7 Leeds …………. (win) the match. They are the best team. We'll know soon when the results are announced. ( )
8 Leeds …………. (win) the match. They were unlucky. ( )
9 Andrew and Chris …………. (return) home yesterday. I hope they aren't lost in Paris. ( )
10 Andrew and Chris …………. (return) home yesterday. We could go and visit them. ( )
11 You …………. (make) me angry. ( )
12 They …………. (make) dinner yet. I'll suggest we go to a restaurant. ( )

4 Rewrite the article**

Rewrite this article making it more certain. The first three lines have been rewritten for you.

The future is here
In the future most people will probably live in very big cities. The countryside could become depopulated as people move to the city looking for work. Many people may find jobs but many others might not. The cities could become overcrowded and polluted. Housing might be difficult to find and could become very expensive. Many people probably won't be able to afford the high city rents. They might be evicted from their homes and join the ever growing influx of people from the countryside living homeless on the streets. Many may become beggars, still more might turn to crime. Others might turn to drugs to escape the pain. They probably won't gain very much from the new consumer capitalism.

A few people will probably be rich. The professional and managerial class ought to do well but the owners of the large multinational companies should comprise the super-rich. They might have country mansions and penthouse apartments in the city. They shouldn't have to worry about the beggars on the streets because they will probably travel by helicopter.

The rest of us will most likely be left down below, desperately trying to survive. Many of us may not.

The future is here

In the future most people will live in very big cities. The countryside will become depopulated as people move to the city looking for work. Many will find jobs but many others won't …

UNIT 15 Requests and Permission: Can I? / Could I? / May I? / Would you mind if I?

USE

ASKING FOR PERMISSION
1 We make requests for permission using *can*:
Can I go out tonight?
2 We also make requests using *could*. This is a more polite form than *can*:
Could I ask a question?
3 We also make requests with *may*. This is more polite and formal than *can* or *could*:
May I use your phone?
4 We also make requests using *Would you mind if ...?* This is the most polite form and is only used for special requests:
Would you mind if I went home early?
5 We can of course ask permission for others:
Can Sylvia come with us?
Could Grandad lie down? He's tired.
May they use the front entrance?
Would you mind if we started without you?

THE RESPONSE: GRANTING PERMISSION
We use *can*, *may* or some other phrases to grant permission (say *yes* to someone's request). Look at the following examples:
Can I go out tonight?
Yes, you can.
Could I ask you a question?
Yes, of course.
May I use your phone?
Certainly, go ahead. / Yes, you may.
Would you mind if I went home early?
No, not at all. / No, of course not.

Note:
May is very formal and not used as often as *can*.
Could is not used to grant permission.
Answering *no* to a *Would you mind if ...?* request grants permission; a *yes* answer would refuse permission.

THE RESPONSE: REFUSING PERMISSION
1 We make polite refusals using *I'm sorry but ...* or *I'm afraid not ...* followed by an explanation:
Could I ask a question?
I'm sorry but we're running late and it's time to close the meeting.
May I use your phone?
I'm afraid not. It's not working.
2 To refuse a *Would you mind if ...* request use *I'm sorry, but ...* or a positive phrase. Remember a negative phrase grants permission.
Would you mind if I went home early?
I'm sorry but we need you here for the meeting.
3 We can make impolite refusals also:
Can I go out tonight?
No. / No, you can't.
Could I ask you a question?
No. / No, you couldn't.
May I use your phone?
No. / No, you may not.
Would you mind if I went home early?
Yes, I would. / Yes, I do mind. / I'm afraid I do.

---

1 Write the dialogue*

Martin and Philip are brothers. Philip is older than Martin and looks after him. Martin wants to do the things listed below. He asks for Philip's permission. Write down the questions he asks. In each case Philip grants permission. Write down his replies. The first two have been done for you.

1 Martin wants to have another of Philip's chocolates.
   Martin: Can *I have another of your chocolates?*
   Philip: *Yes, you can.*
2 Martin wants to use Philip's computer.
   Martin: Could *I use your computer?*
   Philip: *Certainly, go ahead.*
3 Martin wants to stay up late to watch TV.
   Martin: May ....?
   Philip: ....
4 Martin wants to have a lift.
   Martin: Could ....?
   Philip: ....
5 Martin wants to hang his picture above the fireplace.
   Martin: Can ....?
   Philip: ....
6 Martin wants to sit near the fire.
   Martin: May ....?
   Philip: ....
7 Martin wants to make himself a sandwich.
   Martin: Could ....?
   Philip: ....
8 Martin wants to borrow Philip's new tie.
   Martin: Can ....?
   Philip: ....

9   Martin wants to visit Grandma.
    Martin: May .... ?
    Philip: ....
10 Martin wants to play football on Wednesday afternoon.
    Martin: Can .... ?
    Philip: ....
11 Philip is going out. Martin wants to go with him.
    Martin: Can .... ?
    Philip: ....
12 Martin wants to invite Jayne for dinner on Friday evening.
    Martin: Could .... ?
    Philip: ....

2 Choose the correct reply

One week later Martin made the same requests he had made in Exercise 1. This time Philip politely refused to grant permission to Martin. Look at his responses below which are not in the correct order. Write a number next to each one which corresponds to the number of Martin's question in Exercise 1. The first one has been done for you.

(a) I'm sorry but you should be in bed by nine o'clock. (3)
(b) I'm afraid not. I'm going to hang a mirror there. ( )
(c) I'm sorry but there are only a few left and I'd like to save some for our guests. ( )
(d) I'm afraid not. We haven't got any bread. ( )
(e) I'm sorry but I'm having Helen to dinner that night. ( )
(f) I'm afraid not. You must stay in and look after the dog. ( )
(g) I'm sorry but we should let our visitors sit there. ( )
(h) I'm afraid not. She's not well at the moment. ( )
(i) I'm sorry but I want to wear it. ( )
(j) I'm afraid not. The car isn't working very well. ( )
(k) I'm sorry but you've got to be in school on Wednesday afternoon. ( )
(l) I'm afraid not. I need to do some word-processing on it myself. ( )

3 Make requests and answers

Rearrange the words to make requests for permission. Answer the requests by refusing permission impolitely, using the modal in the question.

Examples:
drive / I / can
Can I drive?
No, you can't.
Joanne / could / to you alone / speak
Could Joanne speak to you alone?
No, she couldn't.

1   be / excused / I / may
2   first / can / go / Lynne
3   Gemma / could / have / a biscuit
4   little pussy / may / some milk / have
5   the goldfish / feed / I / can
6   of your time / a minute / could / just have / she
7   the table / may / leave / I
8   the dog / can / the living room / come into
9   I / use / could / your study / to work in
10 into your whereabouts / we / enquire / may
11 to dinner / can / John and Sylvia / come
12 the budgie / let / out of its cage / I / could

4 Rewrite the requests and answers

Look at the requests in Exercise 3. Rewrite them using Would you mind if ...? *Then write responses. Grant permission to the odd numbers (numbers 1, 3, 5, 7, 9 and 11) and refuse permission impolitely to the even numbers (2, 4, 6, 8, 10 and 12).*

Examples:
Can I drive?
Would you mind if I drove?
No, not at all.
Could Joanne speak to you alone?
Would you mind if Joanne spoke to you alone?
Yes, I would mind.

13 use / I / phone / your / may
14 that / could / again / see / you / I
15 summer / study leave / my / during / can / take / I / term / the
16 Harold / work / this / could / help / with / me
17 individually / groups / exercise / instead / can / do / this / we / in / of
18 may / join / you / I / boat / on / trip / the
19 wife / next / could / bring / my / time / I
20 your / may / car / we / evening / borrow / this

UNIT 16 Used to / would / be used to / get used to

USE

USED TO
Used to refers to an action, state or habit in the past which no longer applies or is no longer true:
They **used to dance** so beautifully.
He **used to be a rugby player**, but now he's retired.
I **used to smoke** but I stopped last year.
Note:
When a specific time is mentioned we do not use used to. We do not say:
I **used to walk** to school for five years. (x)
Instead we use the simple past:
I **walked** to school for five years.
USED TO v. BE USED TO / GET USED TO
Be careful not to confuse used to + infinitive with the following: be/get + used to + present participle or noun phrase:
He's **used to working** long hours.
He **got used to** the heat after he moved to Saudi Arabia.
The first example refers to the present while the second refers to the past, but in both cases the meaning is accustomed to or familiar with.
WOULD
1 Would can be used as an alternative to used to:
I **would walk** to school when I was a child.

They **would play** football every weekend.
This is more formal and found mostly in written English.
2 Would is used to show wilfulness or obstinacy on the part of the person being talked about – often used disapprovingly by the speaker:
He **would climb** up the tallest trees, despite what I said.
She **would do** whatever she wanted and nobody could stop her.
He **would say** that, wouldn't he?
In speech, would is often stressed in this use.
3 In the negative would indicates refusal. Because of this you cannot replace didn't use to with wouldn't without changing the meaning. Compare:
He **didn't use to take** the bus to school
He **wouldn't take** the bus to school.
Here wouldn't shows refusal – (He refused to take the bus to school. Didn't he like it? Was it dirty or slow?) and so has a different meaning from didn't use to which is neutral.
Note:
Would cannot replace used to when referring to a past state:
I **would be** a rugby player (x)

1 Write Sentences

Look at the following table containing information about Brendan O'Gara in 1990 and now.

		1990	NOW
1	JOB (be)	dentist	retired
2	HOME (live)	England	Australia
3	STATUS (be)	married	divorced
4	SPORT (play/go)	cricket	surfing
5	DRINK (drink)	tea or coffee	fruit juice
6	FOOD (eat)	fish and chips roast beef	seafood salads
7	NEWSPAPER (read)	The Times	The Australian Outlook
8	EVENING (spend)	watching TV	eating in restaurants
9	WEIGHT (weigh)	100kgs	70kgs
10	HEALTH (be)	unhealthy and fat	healthy and slim
11	MOOD (feel)	sad and stressed	happy and relaxed
12	PERSONALITY (be)	shy	outgoing

Write sentences about what Brendan O'Gara used to do and what he is doing now. Use the verbs in brackets to help you. The first one has been done for you.
1 He used to be a dentist but now he is retired.

2 Complete the story

Complete the story using the past simple, used to or would. Use would wherever possible. The first one has been done for you.

Once upon a time there (1) **was** (be) a beautiful Queen. She (2) .... (stand) in front of the mirror every morning.
When she (3) .... (look) in the mirror she (4) .... (say):
'Mirror, mirror, on the wall
Who is the fairest of them all?'
And the mirror (5) .... (reply): 'You are'.
One morning she (6) .... (ask) her usual question and to her surprise the mirror (7) .... (announce):
'Snow White is the fairest of them all!' So the Queen (8) .... (get) angry and (9) .... (smash) the mirror.
After a hundred evil plots to kill Snow White, and a hundred failures, the Queen (10) .... (give up), (11) .... (retired) and (12) .... (let) Snow White marry the Prince.

UNITS 1–16 Revision Test 1

The questions in Revision Test 1 are about the grammar in Units 1–16.

UNITS 1 – 6

Put the verb in the correct tense.

1 I .... (speak) three languages, including English.
2 I .... (live) in Sardinia for three years. It's beautiful here.
3 I .... (cook) dinner all afternoon. I still haven't finished and I'm already tired.
4 I didn't need to feed the dog because I .... (feed) him earlier.
5 So far, he .... (make) eleven films and we expect he will make many more.
6 Water .... (boil) at 100°C.
7 I .... (not do) anything at the moment.
8 She .... (go) to Brazil in 1997.
9 Where are you from? I .... (come) from Egypt.
10 Andrew .... (play) football when he slipped and broke his leg.

UNITS 7 – 9

Choose the use each sentence shows. Write the number of the sentences in the table.

FIXED FUTURE	
FUTURE ARRANGEMENT	
PREDICTION	
PROMISE	
SUGGESTION	
POLITE ENQUIRY	
VERY NEAR FUTURE	
FUTURE ARRANGEMENT (IN THE PAST)	

11 Will you be working in the study this evening?
12 I will come and see you tomorrow.
13 Bad weather is delaying the take-off. We're going to be late.
14 The match begins at 3.00.
15 They were meeting the following day at 11.00.
16 Quick, sit down! The film's about to start.
17 Shall we go to the races at the weekend?
18 Don't worry. Things will get better.
19 I'm seeing her tonight at 9.00.
20 We will have exhausted our natural mineral resources by the end of the next century if they continue to be exploited at the present rate.

UNIT 10

Read the following sentences ticking ✓ those that can be rewritten in the past with would *and crossing* ✗ *those that cannot. If you have ticked a sentence, say if the meaning changes (Yes or No). If you write yes, say what the change of meaning is.*

21 We used to walk to school when we were children.
22 She used to be a ballet dancer.
23 They got used to the tropical climate rather quickly.
24 I didn't use to go swimming when I was younger.
25 I used to eat meat in the past, but now I'm vegetarian.

UNITS 11 – 16

Complete the sentences by writing the correct modal verb.

26 New recruits .... be in bed at nine and up at six for morning parade. (obligation / rule)
27 He .... play guitar. (ability)
28 I .... do some work. (necessity)
29 You .... talk during exams. (prohibition)
30 Ice-skating .... be exciting. (general possibility)
31 The work .... be completed soon. (probability)
32 .... I borrow your pen? (polite request)
33 I .... hear you. I'm a little deaf. (inability)
34 We .... stay until the end of the party. We can go home early if you wish. (exemption)
35 Bed linen .... be changed every week. (mild obligation)
36 I .... run faster than any of you when I was young. (past ability)
37 Next week's trip .... be interesting. (specific possibility)
38 We .... do what we were told in those days. (past obligation)
39 You .... know the results next week. (future certainty)
40 You should .... reach the top if you stand on the chair. (ability)

UNIT 17   The Third Conditional

FORM

Look at these sentences:
If I **had worked** hard as a young man, I **would have been** rich by now.
If he **had said** he loved her, she **might not have left** him.
If I **hadn't lost** my credit card, we **could have paid** the bill.
If you **hadn't acted** so foolishly, we **wouldn't have got** in such a mess.

We form the third conditional as follows:
 If + past perfect, would (or modal) + present perfect
The order of the clauses may be reversed:
I **would have been** rich by now **if** I **had worked** hard as a young man.
Note:
In spoken English we often shorten the form:
If **I'd worked** hard as a young man, **I'd've been** rich by now.

USE

We use the third conditional to express what might have been the result of a situation if things had been different in the past. It is concerned with what is not true or no longer possible. As such it is commonly used to express regret (first and third examples above), missed opportunities (second example above) or to criticize others (fourth example above). It can also be used to express relief or a positive attitude towards something that did not happen:
If I **hadn't arrived** late at the airport, I **would have been** on the plane that crashed.
It can also be used to make deductions:

If he **had sent** a letter, you **would have received** it already.
(Therefore he did not send a letter)
Note:
In formal English we can put **had** (the auxiliary verb) before the subject to form a conditional:
Had I worked hard as a young man, I **would have been** rich by now. (positive)
Had I **not** lost my credit card, we **could have paid** the bill. (negative)
This form is old-fashioned and more likely to be found in written English than in spoken English.

1 Match the parts

Match the parts in A to the parts in B to express what would have happened if things had been different. The first one has been done for you.

1   If it had rained,
2   If he'd been good,
3   If I had forgotten my watch,
4   If they had sent the letter,
5   If she hadn't hurt her leg,
6   If I had brought my glasses,
7   If I had studied harder,
8   I they had loved each other,
9   If she had worn a seatbelt,
10 If you hadn't lost the pieces,
11 If you had been a member,
12 If my mother had called,

(a) he wouldn't have got into trouble.
(b) she would have survived the crash.
(c) she would have left a message.
(d) I wouldn't have known the time.
(e) I would have noticed the sign.
(f) it would have arrived weeks ago.
(g) we could have played chess.
(h) she could have won the race.
(i) I might have passed the exam.
(j) we might have cancelled the match.
(k) they wouldn't have split up.
(l) they would have let you into the club.

2 Write conditional sentences

Albert is an old man. Here are things he wanted to do, but didn't do. Write conditional sentences to express what Albert could have done if circumstances had been different.

Example:
I wanted to be a doctor, but I didn't have the money to pay for Medical School.
If Albert had had the money to pay for Medical School, he could have been a doctor.

1 I wanted to stay in the countryside, but there was no work.
2 I hoped to find a well-paid job, but I was unskilled.
3 I wanted to marry Mary, but she thought that I was ugly.
4 I tried to be a footballer, but I broke my leg.
5 I thought about moving to France, but I wasn't able to speak French.
6 I tried to start a business but I didn't have enough money.
7 I asked the bank to lend me some money, but they didn't like my business idea.
8 I was offered a job as a life guard, but I wasn't able to swim.
9 I dreamed of being a mountain-climber, but I was afraid of heights.
10 Finally, I planned to rob a bank, but won the lottery and became a millionaire.

3 Complete the dialogue*

Your friend is telling you about what happened to him yesterday. You think he did many foolish things. Complete the dialogue by saying what you would have done if you had been him, using the verb in brackets.

Example:
Friend: Yesterday, I decided to go for a walk. I didn't take my coat even though it was rather cold.
You: If I'd been you, *I'd have taken my coat.* (take)
Friend: When I got to the park, a man asked me the time. I said that I didn't have a watch. He seemed friendly so I began talking to him.

1 You: If I'd been you, ... (begin)
   Friend: The man started asking me a lot of questions and so I sat down beside him on a park bench.
2 You: If I'd been you, ... (sit)
   Friend: He showed me a big silver watch and so I tried it on.
3 You: If I'd been you, ... (try on)
   Friend: He told me it was cheap and I said I wanted to buy it.
4 You: If I'd been you, ... (say)
   Friend: He asked to see my money, so I gave him my wallet.
5 You: If I'd been you, ... (give)
   Friend: He said he would polish the watch for me, so I returned it to him.
6 You: If I'd been you, ... (return)
   Friend: He took the watch and all my money.
7 You: It serves you right. If I'd been you, ... (behave) so stupidly!

4 Write conditional sentences

Write third conditional sentences.
Example:
I / enter the competition / might / win a prize
If I had entered the competition, I might have won a prize.

1 you / study harder / could / pass the exam
2 my father / not be poor / I / might / have a decent education
3 I / not escape his influence / would / be dead by now
4 he / break his leg a week earlier / could not / climb the wall
5 I / arrive sooner / might / save her
6 you / live an honest life / would not / spend half of it in jail
7 a doctor / not be present / I / might / die
8 he / fly to France / would not / have a ferry ticket in his pocket
9 I / go to the interview / might / get the job
10 you / do as you were told / would not / get into trouble
11 I / decide to get divorced / would / be deeply unhappy
12 he / leave before 9.00 / could not / answer the phone at 9.30

5 Choose the use**

Look at your answers to Exercise 4 and choose the use each one shows. Write the number of the sentence in the table. The first one has been done for you.

CRITICISM	*1*
DEDUCTION	
REGRET / MISSED OPPORTUNITY	
RELIEF	

UNIT 18 Conditional: Expressing Possibility 1

FORM

1 Look at these sentences:
*If she works **hard**, she **will pass** the exam.*
*If you **feel** tired, you **can go** to bed.*
*If it's sunny, he **walks** to school.*
Remember how we form conditional sentences.
If + present, *will* (or modal) + base verb
This is usually called the first conditional in traditional grammar.
Another form is:
If + present, main verb in present tense
This is often called the zero conditional in traditional grammar.

2 The order of the clauses may be reversed:
*She **will pass** the exam if she **works** hard.*
*You **can go** to bed if you **feel** tired.*
*He **walks** to school if it's sunny.*

NEGATIVES
Negatives can be placed in the *if* clause or the main clause, or in both, depending upon meaning. Compare:
*If she **doesn't work** hard, she **will fail** the exam.*
*If she **works hard**, she **won't fail** the exam.*
*If she **doesn't work hard**, she **won't pass** the exam.*
The first and third examples have the same meaning, whereas the second suggests a more positive attitude on the part of the speaker.

USE

These conditionals express a possibility for something that usually happens or *(If it's sunny, he walks to school.)* could happen in the future. *(If she works hard, she will pass the exam.* or *If you feel tired, you can go to bed.)* With these conditions, we can
1 express future certainties:
If the weather's bad, they'll cancel the race.
Here, the situation in the main clause is certain to occur if the condition expressed in the *if* clause happens.
2 make suggestions:
*If you **come** by train tomorrow, we **can/could meet** at the station.*
3 state a fact:
*If you **boil** water, it **turns** into steam.*

Note:
another way to state a fact is to use the imperative form:
***Boil** water and it turns into steam.*
4 describe a habit:
*If she **is worried**, she **bites** her fingernails.*
5 express a rule (using *must*):
*If you **come** to school late, you **must report** to the head teacher.*
6 express possibilities (using *can* or *could*):
*If the weather's fine at the weekends, we **can/could go** to the beach.*

Note:
1 Uses 2 and 6 are often very similar, so be careful that you do not confuse them.

Note:
2 In 4, 5 and 6, we can replace *if* with *whenever*.

---

1 Match the parts**

Match the parts in **A** with the ones in **B**. Then state whether the sentence is a suggestion or a possibility. The first one has been done for you.

A
1 If you are lucky,
2 If there's a movie on tonight,
3 If the party's finished,
4 If you don't take a map,
5 If the telephone rings,
6 If the telephone rings,

B
(a) you could take a message.
(b) we can go home.
(c) you can get lost.
(d) it could be for me.
(e) we could go and watch it.
(f) you could win a prize

1 = possibility

---

2 Write sentences

Write sentences to express a future certainty. Remember to put the verbs into the correct tense/form.

Examples:
the game / they / win / champions / be
If they win the game, they will be champions.
eat / get / too much / she / fat
She will get fat if she eats too much.

1 take / you / get / your medicine / better
2 become / save / you / your money / rich
3 the car / we / start / go / London
4 the bus / my appointment / be / miss / late / I
5 cause / you / do / an accident / that
6 be / punished / you / misbehave
7 break / be not / vase / you / careful
8 fly / first class / win / lottery / I
9 not / he / succeed / waste / time
10 the job / the salary / she / low / not / be / take

3 Rewrite the sentences

These sentences are statements of fact in the imperative form. Rewrite them in conditional form. Use the pronoun you *in each case.*

Example:
Go to Tokyo, and it's always crowded.
If you go to Tokyo, it's always crowded.

1 Live in the countryside and life is quiet.
2 Polish silver and it shines.
3 Go to the theatre on Wednesdays and there is opera.
4 Eat sweets and they damage your teeth.
5 Touch marble and it feels cool.
6 Add salt and it improves the flavour.
7 Burn incense and it smells sweet.
8 Take the motorway and there is a lot of traffic.

4 Complete the sentences*

Paul is interviewing Anna about her morning routine. Read the dialogue and then complete the sentences using a conditional form.

Paul: Can you tell me about your day, Anna?
Anna: Well, when I'm working the alarm goes off at seven.
Paul: And if you're not working?
Anna: Oh, I stay in bed till lunch time.
Paul: And do you have anything to eat in the morning?
Anna: I usually have toast for breakfast, although I don't eat anything when I'm dieting, which is quite often.
Paul: What time do you leave home?
Anna: At eight, or as soon as I can afterwards, as I'm not always ready by then.
Paul: And how do you go to work?
Anna: I usually walk.
Paul: Even if it's raining like today?
Anna: Well, if it's raining, I take the bus. Or my umbrella.

Paul: What time do you start work?
Anna: Eight-thirty.
Paul: And are you ever late?
Anna: Well, every time I'm late the boss gets angry, so I try to be on time.
Paul: And what's the first thing you do at work?
Anna: I listen to the answering machine and note down the messages for the manager. If he's not there, the first thing I do is make myself a cup of coffee.

Example:
The alarm goes off at seven ....
The alarm goes off at seven if Anna is working.

1 Anna stays in bed till lunch time
   ....
2 .... she leaves after eight.
3 .... she takes the bus.
4 Anna's boss gets angry ....
5 Anna has a cup of coffee ....

5 Choose the Use*

Read the sentence below and choose the use of the conditional each sentence shows. Write the number of the sentence in the table. The first one has been done for you.

FUTURE CERTAINTY	
SUGGESTION	*1*
FACT	
HABIT	
RULE	
POSSIBILITY	

1 If you're not too tired, we can go jogging.
2 If you fail the exam, you won't get a place at university.
3 If you forget, I will remind you.
4 If he's in a hurry, he runs to school.
5 If you diet, you lose weight.
6 If he sees her, he loses his temper.
7 If you break anything, you must pay for it.
8 If you do the lottery, you can win a fortune.
9 If you pot the black in snooker, you get seven points.
10 If you don't stop it, I'll get angry.
11 If you help her, she'll be grateful.
12 If you make a promise, you must keep it.
13 If the audience doesn't laugh, we change the jokes.

UNIT 19 Conditional: Expressing Possibility 2

FORM

Look at these sentences:
If she **worked** hard, she **would pass** the exam.
If you **felt** tired, you **could go** to bed.
If it **was** sunny, he **walked** to school.

In addition to the forms in Unit 18, we can make the possible conditional in the following ways:
If + past, would (or modal) + base verb
If + past, main verb in past tense

USE

IF + PAST, *WOULD* (OR MODAL) + BASE VERB
We use this conditional to express a real possibility in the future:
If the weather was bad, they **would cancel** the race.
This is similar to a form of conditional discussed in Unit 18:
If the weather's bad, they'**ll cancel** the race. (Example 10 in Unit 18)
There is a difference, however, between these two examples. In the first, the speaker feels the possibility expressed in the *if* clause is less likely than in the second.

IF + PAST, MAIN VERB IN PAST TENSE
We use this conditional to describe a state or habit in the past:
If she **was** worried, she **bit** her fingernails.
This is also similar to a form of conditional discussed in Unit 18:

If she **is** worried, she **bites** her fingernails.
Again, there is a difference between these two forms. In the first, the use of the past means that the habit (biting her fingernails) belongs to the past. In the second, the present tense means a general habit that does not belong to any particular time.

Note:
1 With this form of conditional *if* can be replaced by *when*, *whenever* or *each time*:
Whenever it **was** sunny, he **walked** to school.
Each time she **was** worried, she **bit** her fingernails.

Note:
2 The conditional form of *if* + past, *would* (or modal) + base verb can also be used to describe a habit in the past:
If she **was** worried, she **would bite** her fingernails.
Here, *would* has the same meaning as *used to*. (See Unit 16)

1 Match the parts

Match the parts in **A** to the ones in **B** in order to express future possibilities. The first one has been done for you.

A
1   If he recovered by Thursday,
2   If it snowed tomorrow,
3   If she changed her job,
4   If you bought her a ring,
5   If you were more friendly,
6   If we reduced the price,
7   If you ate more vegetables,
8   If somebody else volunteered,
9   If we sold more items,
10 If she returned next week,
11 If we gave him some money,
12 If we promised to behave,

B
(a) she'd get more money.
(b) profits would rise.
(c) you would feel healthier.
(d) she might agree to marriage.
(e) he could be in the team.
(f) they'd cancel the fair.
(g) we would sell more items.
(h) he might leave us alone.
(i) people would like you.
(j) you could give up the job.
(k) they might let us go out.
(l) the show could begin.

2 Write conditional sentences

Write conditional sentences to express a future possibility.

Example:
I / improved / the weather / to the beach / go
If the weather improved, I'd go to the beach.

1. she / the contest / be happy / won
2. be shocked / he / you / telephoned him
3. ate / feel sick / you / that
4. worked / you / overtime / earn / more money
5. stopped / you / we / hear / talking / the radio
6. she / go / passed / to college / the exams
7. dieted / you / lose weight
8. that / did / I / be angry / you
9. told her / tell everybody / you / she
10. went quietly / you / not / they / be disturbed

3 Find the conditionals (Past Habits and Actions)*

Phil and Kim went to school together as children. They are now adults and have not seen each other for many years. Underline the conditional sentences in the dialogue. (There are ten.) The first one has been done for you.

Phil: Do you remember music classes with Mr Nightingale?
Kim: The one with the funny face? Oh, yes, I remember him: he had the most awful expressions.
Phil: <u>Yes, if he was playing happy songs, he had a ridiculous smile on his face.</u>
Kim: And if he was playing sad songs, he started to cry.
Phil: Whenever the headmaster came into class, Nightingale would bow!
Kim: And each time the headmaster asked Mr Nightingale a question, he would answer: 'Yes, sir! Yes, sir! Yes, sir!'
Phil: Bowing all the time!
Kim: And wasn't the headmaster awful.
Phil: If you arrived late, he shouted: 'Report to my office, at break!'
Kim: And if you weren't neatly dressed, he sent you home.
Phil: And if you forgot your tie, he'd punish you.
Kim: He was always getting angry with you for forgetting your tie.
Phil: Well, my brother had lost his tie and whenever he could, he took mine, so I was often without one.
Kim: And that explains why whenever the headmaster came into class, you would look down at your book.
Phil: Yes; each time he came in I stared straight down. I was praying that he wouldn't notice my tie was missing!
Kim: Ah, the good old days ...

4 Choose the conditional

Look at the answers to Exercise 3 and choose which box they belong to. The first one has been done for you.

If + past + *would* + verb stem	If + past + verb, past tense
	1 If he was playing happy songs he had a ridiculous smile on his face.

5 Choose the use**

Look at the table below and then choose the use each conditional sentence shows. Write the number of the sentence in the correct place in the table. The first one has been done for you. This exercise applies to both this and the previous unit.

1. If you read newspapers, you are aware of current events.
2. If you play with fire, you'll get burnt.
3. If you got lost, you would sit down and cry.
4. If you cook the dinner, I'll do the washing up.
5. If you are happy, you always smile.
6. If you got sick, you got really sick.
7. If you were ill, you wouldn't be able to go.
8. If you are ill, you'll miss the game.
9. If you burn paper, it produces smoke.
10. If you told a lie, you might feel guilty.
11. If you leave early, you must inform your supervisor.
12. If you made a mess, your mother would shout at you.

FUTURE CERTAINTY	
POSSIBILITY	
SUGGESTION	
FACT	*1*
PAST HABIT	
GENERAL HABIT	
RULE	

UNIT 20 Conditional: Expressing the Impossible or Unreal

FORM

1 Look at these sentences:
If I were rich, I would buy a house.
If you had a car, we could drive to London.
Remember how we form the impossible or hypothetical (unreal) conditional:
If + past, *would* (or modal) + base verb
This is usually called the second conditional in traditional grammar.

2 Look at these sentences:
If I were rich, I would have bought a house.
If you had a car, we could have driven to London.
We can also form the impossible/unreal conditional as follows:
If + past, *would* (or modal) + present perfect

3 Look at this sentence:
If I had worked hard as a young man, I would be rich.
We can also form the impossible/unreal conditional as follows:
If + past perfect, *would* (or modal) + base verb

4 Look at this sentence:
If I had been rich, I would have bought the house.
We can also form the impossible/unreal conditional as follows:
If + past perfect, *would* (or modal) + present perfect
This is usually called the third conditional in traditional grammar. See Unit 17.

USE

IF + PAST, *WOULD* (OR MODAL) + BASE VERB
We use this conditional to express an imagined situation which is impossible or unreal in the present or impossible/improbable in the future:
If she was a man, she would be the manager by now.
(But she isn't a man, so she isn't the manager.)
If I won a million dollars, I would go on a world cruise.
(But I probably won't win, so I'll have to stay home.)
Note:
This form is the same as a possible conditional form (see Unit 19). Whether the form is used as a possible or impossible/unreal conditional should be clear from the situation in which the sentence is used.
Note:
With the past form of the verb *to be*, we often use *were* instead of *was* in the *if* clause. *Were* is considered more correct, but *was* is used informally. With the first person singular, however, we normally use *were*, especially in the phrase *If I were you* ...

IF + PAST, *WOULD* (OR MODAL) + PRESENT PERFECT

1 We use this conditional to express an imagined situation which is impossible or unreal in the present or impossible or improbable in the future:
If she was a man, she would have been the manager by now.
If you had a car, we could have driven to London next week.

2 We can use this conditional form to refer to the past:
If you had a car, we could have driven to London last week.
(But you don't have a car, so we didn't drive to London last week.)
If I were rich, I would have bought a house last year.
(But I'm not rich, so I didn't buy a house last year.)

IF + PAST PERFECT, *WOULD* (OR MODAL) + BASE VERB
We use this conditional to express an unreal situation in the past and its present or future consequences:
If I had been healthy, I would be happy.
(But I haven't been healthy, so I'm not happy.)
If I had been healthy, I would be running the marathon at this moment.
(But I haven't been healthy, so I'm not running the marathon.)
If I had been healthy, I would run the marathon next week.
(But I haven't been healthy, so I won't run the marathon next week.)

IF + PAST PERFECT, *WOULD* (OR MODAL) + PRESENT PERFECT
We normally use this form of conditional to express an unreal situation in the past and its past consequences:
If I had been healthy, I would have run the marathon.
(But I wasn't healthy, so I didn't run the marathon.)
It can also be used, however, to refer to present or future consequences:
If I had been rich, I would have bought the house next year.
See Unit 17 for a more detailed discussion of this form of conditional.

1 Match the sentences

Match the following to express an imagined (unreal) situation. The first one has been done for you.

A
1. If I had the time,
2. If she played tennis,
3. If he was a Mormon,
4. If they were older,
5. If my mother were alive,
6. If China were in Europe,
7. If you played chess,
8. If he was smaller,
9. If she liked coffee,
10. If she wasn't a vegetarian,
11. If I owned a television,
12. If I had some money,

B
(a) I would fight him.
(b) I might visit it.
(c) she would have been 100 next year.
(d) I would write a book.
(e) I would not have made tea last night.
(f) she would have entered the competition.
(g) I would have watched the football match last night.
(h) I would have cooked beef tomorrow.
(i) I would have bought a ticket for the football match tomorrow.
(j) you would have understood how the champion beat his opponent.
(k) they could go to the disco.
(l) he could have two wives.

2 Choose the form

Look at your answers to Exercise 1 and choose the form each conditional shows. Write the number of the sentence in the table.

IF + PAST, WOULD (OR MODAL) + BASE VERB	1
IF + PAST, WOULD (OR MODAL) + PRESENT PERFECT	

3 Explain the use

Now say if the main clause refers to the past, or to some time in the present or future. The first one has been done for you.

1 The main clause refers to some time in the present or future.

4 Choose the use

Read the sentences below and choose the use each one shows. Write the number of the sentence in the table. This exercise applies to uses from Units 17, 18, 19 and 20. The first one has been done for you.

UNREAL PAST + PAST CONSEQUENCE	1
UNREAL PAST + PRESENT CONSEQUENCE	
UNREAL PAST + FUTURE CONSEQUENCE	
IMPOSSIBLE/UNREAL PRESENT	
IMPOSSIBLE/IMPROBABLE FUTURE	
DEDUCTION	
PAST HABIT	
HABIT	
FUTURE CERTAINTY	
FUTURE POSSIBILITY	

1 If you hadn't sworn at the manager, you wouldn't have lost your job.
2 When he was depressed, he would lock himself in his room for hours.
3 If the money is good, I'll take the job.
4 If the winter hadn't been so cold, the flowers would be out by now.
5 If sales increased, we would expand the business.
6 If she had lost her passport, she couldn't have boarded the plane.
7 If she is angry, she doesn't speak for days.
8 If I were you, I would go.
9 If his childhood had been more normal, he wouldn't be going to jail next week.
10 When he was nervous, his hands shook.
11 If you had a television, we could have watched tomorrow's concert.
12 If we had more money, we could have taken a plane to Dublin last week.
12 If I had danced more confidently, I might have been chosen for the musical.
13 If he was a woman, he would understand.
14 If Bruce had been more charming, he might have maried a more beautiful woman than Sheila.

UNIT 21 — unless v. if not

USE

Unless and *if not* are negative conditionals. We use them to state an exception to what we are saying.
1 We use both *unless* and *if not* with possible conditionals:
Terry goes running every morning, **unless** it is raining.
Terry goes running every morning, **if** it **isn't** raining.
2 *If not* and *unless* are also often used to give advice, to criticize or warn:
Unless you study harder, you will fail your exams.
If you **don't** study harder, you will fail your exams.
3 With impossible or unreal conditionals we use *if not*. *Unless* is either wrong or unusual in these conditionals:
Terry would have gone running **if** it **hadn't** rained.
If I **weren't** poor, I would buy a castle.

Note:
When we want to give advice / criticize / warn we can replace *if not* and *unless* by a modal verb such as *should* or *must*, or by the imperative form:
You **should** study harder or you will fail your exams.
You **must** study harder otherwise you will fail your exams.
Study harder or you will fail your exams.

1 Match the parts

Match the parts in A to the ones on B to make sentences. The first one has been done for you.

A
1 We'll have Chinese food,
2 I work at home on Thursdays,
3 We play golf every weekend,
4 He sings at the local club,
5 I will switch the music off,
6 She doesn't wear make-up,
7 They picnic most summer weekends,
8 He won't do a thing,
9 We'll go to the cinema,
10 George will give you a lift,
11 I won't help you,
12 Sheila can do the shopping,

B
(a) unless she doesn't want to.
(b) unless you turn down the volume.
(c) unless you pay him.
(d) unless the Indian restaurant is open.
(e) unless the course is flooded.
(f) unless you help me.
(g) unless a guest band is playing.
(h) unless his car is full.
(i) unless she's meeting a boy.
(j) unless I have a meeting at the office.
(k) unless the weather prevents them.
(l) unless we can get a seat at the theatre.

2 Rewrite the sentences

Rewrite the sentences from Exercise 1 using if not. *The first one has been done for you.*

1 We'll have Chinese food if the Indian restaurant isn't open.

Examples:
She would have gone abroad for her holiday if the exchange rate hadn't changed.
(not possible)
He goes for a walk in the evening if there isn't a film on television.
(possible) *He goes for a walk in the evening unless there is a film on television.*

3 Rewrite the sentences

Read the following sentences and decide whether or not it is possible to rewrite them using unless. *If it is possible, then rewrite the sentence.*

1 If you don't hurry, you'll miss the train.
2 If you weren't so lazy, you would be top of the class.
3 If you hadn't lost your licence, we could have gone by car.
4 You won't live beyond sixty, if you don't stop smoking.

5 If you don't set off before seven, you'll get caught in the traffic.
6 If he didn't like the food, he should have said so.
7 If I hadn't failed the exam, I could be manager by now.
8 They went sailing every summer, if they weren't short of money.
9 They wouldn't have got into such a mess if they hadn't behaved like fools.
10 We made our own breakfast if mother hadn't already done so.
11 I would go myself if I weren't ill.
12 He would talk for hours if he wasn't feeling ill.

4 Rewrite the sentences

Rewrite the sentences using unless *and* if not.
Example:
You must stop doing that, otherwise I'll be angry.
Unless you stop doing that, I'll be angry.
If you don't stop doing that, I'll be angry.

1 You must finish your dinner or you can't have any pudding.
2 You must listen carefully otherwise you'll forget.
3 You must chew your food thoroughly or you'll get indigestion.
4 You must wear a suit and tie, otherwise they won't let you in.
5 You must take the proper equipment, otherwise you'll put the expedition in danger.
6 You must answer all the questions or you will lose marks.
7 You must take care or you'll hurt yourself.
8 You must believe me, otherwise nobody will.
9 You must behave well or you'll disgrace us.
10 You must bring a sandwich otherwise you'll be hungry.
11 You must tell the manager, or you'll get into trouble.
12 You must book your hotel in advance, otherwise you might not get a room.

5 Rewrite the sentences

Rewrite the sentences from Exercise 4 using the imperative form.
Example:
Stop doing that, otherwise I'll be angry.

6 Write sentences

Here are the rules for La Exotica Night Club and Casino. Write sentences to explain the consequences of breaking the rules. The first one has been done for you.

LA EXOTICA NIGHT CLUB AND CASINO
NOTICE TO MEMBERS

Please note: **Club members are required to:**
(1) be over 21 years of age
(2) be recommended by another member
(3) pay a yearly membership fee of £150
(4) dress smartly
(5) behave respectfully towards other members
(6) pay for all purchases in cash
(7) vacate club premises by 3.00 a.m.
(8) sign in all non-member guests
(9) be responsible for guests' actions
(10) obey the rules
(11) follow any additional instructions of the House Manager
(12) know the safety regulations and location of fire exits

1 (if not) *If you are not over 21 years of age* .. you cannot become a member
2 (unless) .... you cannot join the club.
3 (must) .... or your membership will be revoked.
4 (should) .... or you may be refused entry.
5 (should) .... or you will be asked to leave.
6 (if not) .... your membership will be revoked.
7 (imperative) .... or you may be removed physically.
8 (must) .... or they will not be permitted to enter.
9 (imperative) .... or you may be excluded from the club.
10 (unless) .... your membership will be revoked.
11 (imperative) .... or you may be excluded from the club.
12 (if not) .... you could be a danger to yourself and others.

UNIT 22 Wishing

FORM and USE

We wish when we want something. We can wish about the past, present or future. Wishing expresses a regret for the state of things as they were, are, or (probably) will be and a hope that they might be different.
Wishing can express strong feelings which we can show in the stress and quality of the speaker's voice.

WISHING ABOUT THE PRESENT
To wish about the present we use PRESENT + PAST. Look at the following table:

PRESENT	PAST
I wish	I were in Paris now.
If only	they had more money.
	she wasn't so awkward.
	I could swim.

WISHING ABOUT THE FUTURE
To wish about the future we use PRESENT + PAST CONTINUOUS or PRESENT + COULD / WOULD. Look at the following table:

PRESENT	PAST CONTINUOUS
I wish	she was coming to the party next week.
	they weren't meeting us in London tomorrow.
	COULD OR WOULD
If only	you could help Andrew on Friday.
	the committee would decide quickly.

Note:
With the past form of the verb *to be*, we often use *were* instead of *was* in the *wish* clause. *Were* is considered more correct, but *was* is used more informally.

WISHING ABOUT THE PAST
To wish about the past we use PRESENT + PAST PERFECT. Look at the following table:

PRESENT	PAST PERFECT
I wish	you had listened to me.
	I hadn't spent the money.
If only	she had been more helpful.

Note:
Could is used when wishing about the present and the future. When wishing about the present *could* = past of *can*.

1 Make wishes

Make wishes about the past.
Example:
they / answer / my letter
I wish they had answered my letter.

1 the cat / come / home
2 she / go / to the fair
3 the government / change / the law
4 she / fall in love / with me
5 the sun / shine
6 he / get / a new job
7 they / not close / the local cinema
8 you / buy / a new car
9 she / not bring / her husband
10 they / not do / that
11 the children / not cause / so much trouble
12 Julie / be / my friend

2 Make wishes

Look at your answers to Exercise 1. Make these wishes about the past into wishes about the future.
Example:
I wish they had answered my letter.
I wish they would answer my letter.

3 Write sentences

Here is information about Sarah Smith and about what she wants to be or do. Write sentences expressing the wishes she makes. The first one has been done for you.

	REALITY Sarah ...	WISHES Sarah wants to ...
1	is called Sarah Smith.	be called Rosie Rage.
2	is 15 years old.	be 18 years old.
3	has straight brown hair.	have curly red hair.
4	is short.	be tall.
5	is unknown.	be famous.
6	is a singer in her school choir.	be a pop singer.
7	lives with her parents.	live in her own apartment.
8	rides a bicycle.	drive a sports car.
9	doesn't have a boyfriend.	have lots of boyfriends.
10	wears school uniform.	wear skin-tight leathers.
11	goes on holiday to Brighton.	go on holiday abroad.
12	earns £30 a week in her part-time job.	earn millions.

1 *I wish I was called Rosie Rage instead of being called Sarah Smith.*

Answers

UNIT 1
Exercise 1
1 a 2 b 3 a 4 b 5 b 6 a 7 a 8 a 9 b 10 a 11 b 12 a 13 b 14 a 15 a = Catherine is already a mother. 15 b = Catherine is pregnant.

Exercise 2

PRESENT STATE: LONG TERM	3
PRESENT STATE: TEMPORARY	5
PRESENT STATE: MOMENT OF SPEAKING (STATE VERBS)	7, 8, 12, 13
ACTIVITY IN PROGRESS / TEMPORARY PROCESS	2, 4, 9, 15b
HABIT / REGULAR HAPPENINGS	11
FACT / GENERAL TRUTH	1, 6, 10, 14, 15a

UNIT 2
Exercise
1 was shining 2 were singing 3 felt 4 was walking or walked 5 stopped 6 took 7 thought or was thinking 8 walked 9 was pouring 10 were picking up 11 dropping off 12 were speeding 13 were having 14 watched 15 stumbled 16 were looking 17 stepping 18 seemed 19 was coming 20 stared 21 changed 22 turned 23 managed 24 was climbing 25 rushed 26 was holding or held 27 removed 28 opened 29 were 30 gasped 31 demanded 32 said 33 was walking 34 shot 35 faded

UNIT 3
Exercise 1
1 have / saw 2 haven't finished 3 arrived 4 have 5 haven't / flew 6 has / put 7 haven't sold 8 hasn't / hasn't cleaned 9 have / told 10 have / have discussed *or* discussed

Exercise 2
2 went 3 had 4 have ... (ever) been 5 have visited 6 have travelled 7 did ... see 8 went 9 spent 10 flew 11 swam 12 were 13 Have...swum 14 went 15 did ... think 16 was 17 were 18 Have ... sat 19 Weren't 20 was 21 have ... been 22 did ... do 23 said 24 was 25 showed 26 assured 27 called 28 was 29 offered 30 agreed 31 have ... known 32 Have ... told 33 approached 34 lowered

Exercise 3
1 a 2 b 3 b 4 b 5 b 6 a 7 b 8 b 9 a 10 b 11 a 12 a

Exercise 4

PAST (FINISHED) EVENT	12
REGULARLY OCCURRING PAST EVENTS	6, 9
PAST (FINISHED) EVENT + FOR	11
PAST EVENT + PAST ADVERBIAL	1
PRESENT EFFECT OF PAST EVENTS	5, 7
UNFINISHED PAST EVENT	4
UNFINISHED EVENT + FOR/SINCE	2, 8, 10
PAST EVENT + PERFECT ADVERBIAL	3

UNIT 4
1 Joyce has been doing the washing up.
2 Andrew and Chris have been cleaning the car.
3 Michael has been cooking the dinner.
4 Joseph and Daniel have been swimming.
5 I have been working all day.
6 Catherine and Hugh have been dancing the tango.
7 You have been studying hard.
8 Martin has been staying up late every night.
9 We have been decorating the living room.
10 The actors have been giving an exhausting performance.
11 Hannah has been climbing a mountain.
12 The porter has been carrying bags all day long.

Exercise 2
1 have you been travelling 2 Have you been practising 3 have you been doing 4 have you been listening 5 Have you been reading

Exercise 3
1 ✓ 2 ✗ 3 ✓ 4 ✗ 5 ✓ 6 ✗ 7 ✗ 8 ✓ 9 ✗ 10 ✓ 11 ✗ 12 ✓

Exercise 4
1 had 2 have been considering 3 travelled 4 was 5 have not been having 6 have been meaning 7 appeared 8 have been appearing 9 didn't remember 10 have been remembering 11 have benn going 12 went

Exercise 5
1 producing 2 preparing 3 talking 4 coming 5 intending 6 writing 7 waiting 8 celebrating 9 raining 10 travelling 11 ignoring 12 wandering

UNIT 5
Exercise 1
1 have increased rapidly 2 have decreased rapidly 3 have increased rapidly 4 have remained steady 5 have decreased steadily

Exercise 2
1 have been shouting 2 have run 3 has written 4 have done 5 have broken 6 have you been doing 7 have been writing / have reached 8 Have ... read 9 has been staring 10 have answered

Exercise 3
A dense cloud of smoke <u>has descended</u> over parts of South-East Asia. The smoke <u>has led</u> to a fall in daytime visibility which now is as little as five metres. People <u>have been wearing</u> masks to aid breathing. The vulnerable - especially the very old and very young - <u>have been suffering</u> the awful consequences of the smoke on their health. Patients <u>have been waiting</u> outside hospitals unable to cope with the growing numbers of the sick and dying. The Indonesian Government <u>has declared</u> a state of national emergency and <u>has told</u> people to stay indoors.
Environmental and wildlife protection groups <u>have declared</u> this the greatest environmental catastrophe for decades and warn the repercussions are not simply national but international as the smoke gradually spreads its way across South-East Asia and the globe.

Exercise 4

PRESENT PERFECT	PRESENT PERFECT CONTINUOUS
has descended	(has been descending)
has led	(has been leading)
(have worn)	have been wearing
(have suffered)	have been suffering
(have waited)	have been waiting
has declared	(has been declaring)
has told	(has been telling)
have declared	(have been declaring)

Exercise 5
1 have ... been doing 2 Have ... been jogging 3 have been cooking 4 have been working 5 have ... finished 6 have prepared 7 have put 8 haven't made 9 has ... been cooking 10 has been roasting 11 have had 12 have been trying 13 haven't eaten 14 have been dreaming 15 has been boiling

UNIT 6
Exercise 1
1 h 2 g 3 i 4 f 5 b 6 j 7 c 8 e 9 d 10 a

Exercise 2
1 After he had done the gardening he had a bath.
2 After the police had investigated the crime they arrested the criminal.
3 After she had written a novel she became famous.
4 After he had eaten he did the washing up.
5 After we had sold the car we took the bus.
6 After they had made a collection they counted the money.
7 After the girl had had a bath she went to bed.
8 After I had saved enough money I bought a car.
9 After the accident had happened the ambulance arrived.
10 After the campers had collected the wood they lit a fire.

Exercise 3
1 have captured 2 arrested 3 heard 4 had already heard 5 rang out 6 arrived 7 had called / called 8 had shot / shot 9 had fallen out 10 had attempted / was attempting 11 turned 12 caught 13 was trying 14 discovered 15 had stolen 16 issued 17 have solved 18 have caught 19 has done 20 have never known

Exercise 4

	Past Perfect	Present Perfect	Past Simple	Past Continuous
		have captured		
			arrested	
			heard	
	had already heard			
			rang out	
			arrived	
	had called		called	
	had shot			
	had fallen out			
	had attempted			was attempting
			turned	
			caught	
				was trying
			discovered	
	had stolen			
			issued	
		have solved		
		have caught		
		has done		
		have never known		

UNIT 7
Exercise 1
1 am having 2 does ... close 3 Is...seeing 4 am taking 5 takes 6 begins

Exercise 2
1 is to visit 2 am about to leave 3 are about to enter 4 am about to 5 is to announce 6 are to meet

Exercise 3
1 d 2 e 3 a 4 h 5 j 6 c 7 i 8 b 9 f 10 f or g

Exercise 4

PREDICTION	4
PREDICTION WITH EVIDENCE	1, 5
REQUEST	2, 8
SUGGESTION	3
DECISION MADE AT THE MOMENT OF SPEAKING	7, 10(g)
DECISION MADE BEFORE SPEAKING	6, 9(f)

Exercise 5
1 Will...be going 2 Will...be driving 3 will be supervising 4 will be leading 5 Will...be staying

UNIT 8
Exercise 1
1 She was about to close the shop when a customer entered. 2 The pilot was about to take off when the emergency light came on. 3 James was about to go out when Paul called round. 4 He was about to knock when the door opened. 5 I was about to take the dog for a walk when it started raining.

Exercise 2
1 a & d / b & c 2 a & d / b & c 3 a & c / b & d 4 a & c / b & d 5 a & c / b & d 6 a & d / b & c

Exercise 3
1 c 2 f 3 j 4 e 5 b 6 a 7 d 8 i 9 h 10 g 11 l 12 k

Exercise 4

UNFULFILLED INTENTION	2, 5, 10, 11
INTERRUPTED (INTENDED) ACTION	1, 4, 6, 8
FUTURE PLAN (IN PAST) UNFULFILLED	3, 7, 9, 12

Exercise 5
1 John Keats was going to be a surgeon but he actually became a poet.
2 Mahatma Gandhi was going to be a barrister but he actually became a spiritual leader. 3 Adolf Hitler was going to be a painter but he actually became a politician. 4 Sigmund Freud was going to be a scientist but he actually became a psychoanalyst.
5 H.G. Wells was going to be a zoologist but he actually became a writer.
6 Ludwig Wittgenstein was going to be a pilot but he actually became a philosopher. 7 James Joyce was going to be a priest but he actually became a writer. 8 Che Guevara was going to be a doctor but he actually became a revolutionary. 9 Joseph Stalin was going to be a monk but he actually became a politician. 10 Albert Einstein was going to be a violinist but he actually became a physicist.

UNIT 9
Exercise 1
1 No, my contract won't have expired by April. It'll have expired by May.
2 No, I / we won't have moved house by Christmas. I / We'll have moved house by Easter.
3 No, I won't have bought a new car by summer. I'll have bought a new car by winter.
4 No, I won't have paid you by this Friday. I'll have paid you by next Friday.
5 No, you won't have received it by next week. You'll have received it by the week after next.

6 No, he won't have recovered before the holidays. He'll have recovered by the end of the holidays.
7 No, I won't have repaired it by this afternoon. I'll have repaired it by this evening.
8 No, the company won't have expanded by next year. It'll have expanded by the year after next.
9 No, the rains won't have stopped by next week. They'll have stopped by next month.
10 No, I / we won't have completed the project by 2010. We'll have completed the project by 2020.
11 No, he won't have reached base camp by tomorrow. He'll have reached base camp by the day after tomorrow.
12 No, I won't have done it by the time you arrive. I'll have done it by the time you leave.

Exercise 2
1 It is estimated that sales of children's books will have risen to 6,500 by 2010.
2 It is estimated that sales of novels will have fallen to 15,000 by 2010.
3 It is estimated that sales of biographies will have risen to 7,000 by the year 2010.
4 It is estimated that sales of schools books will not have changed by the year 2010.
5 It is estimated that sales of academic books will have risen to 3000 by the year 2010.
6 It is estimated that sales of audio books will have risen to 3000 by the year 2010.
7 It is estimated that sales of factual books will have not have changed by the the year 2010.
8 It is estimated that sales of reference books will have fallen to 300 by the year 2010.
9 It is estimated that sales of special interest books will have risen to 1,500 by the year 2010.
10 It is estimated that sales of comics will have ceased by the year 2010.
11 It is estimated that sales of magazines will have risen to 10,000 by the year 2010.
12 It is estimated that sales of newspapers will not have changed by the year 2010.

Exercise 3
1 will have closed 2 will have declined 3 will have studied 4 will have overtaken 5 will have risen 6 will have disappeared 7 will have gone 8 will have replaced 9 will have melted 10 will have widened 11 will have spent 12 will have died

Exercise 4
1 I'll have earned, 2 will you have done, 3 I'll have finished, 4 I'll have helped, 5 will you have continued, 6 will have gone, 7 Will it have paid, 8 I'll have received, 9 will have had to, 10 I'll have thought, 11 I'll have found

UNIT 10
Exercise 1
1 You mustn't run in the pool area.
2 You mustn't jump in the pool area.
3 You mustn't fight in the pool area.
4 You mustn't duck people.
5 You shouldn't shout as it can detract attention from a real emergency.
6 Those with serious health problems should consult their doctor before swimming.
7 You should allow at least half an hour after eating a large meal before swimming.
8 You shouldn't swim after drinking alcohol.
9 You should notify the attendant immediately in the event of an emergency.
10 You mustn't attempt life saving unless you are qualified to do so.
11 Children under 10 years old mustn't swim unless accompanied by an adult.
12 You must not smoke in the pool area.

Exercise 2

OBLIGATION	3, 4, 10, 11, 14, 19, 20
MILD (AVOIDABLE) OBLIGATION	2, 12, 13
PAST OBLIGATION	1, 8
PAST (UNOBSERVED) OBLIGATION	6
PROHIBITION	9, 16
MILD PROHIBITION	5, 18
EXEMPTION	7, 15, 17

Exercise 3
1 You have to wear a suit and tie for work now. (No change.)
2 You should have written and thanked people who sent you birthday presents. (In the past this is an unobserved obligation.)
3 You had to do your homework. (An order becomes a recollection.)
4 He had to leave yesterday. (No change.)
5 She shouldn't have gone out alone after dark. (Advice becomes a reprimand or the expression of a worry.)
6 We should finish the job in two days time. (Failure to carry out a past obligation becomes a prediction.)
7 You didn't have to go. (No change.)
8 In the army you have to polish your boots until you can see your face in them. (No change.)
9 (Not possible.)
10 Factory employees had to stamp their time cards on arrival. (No change.)
11 Women had to wear a veil over their faces in some Muslim countries. (No change.)
12 All people should have had equal rights in a fair society. (This becomes an unobserved obligation in the past.)
13 (Not possible to change a general notice to the past without it seeming strange.)
14 The treasurer had to attend all meetings relating to finance. (No change.)
15 The treasurer didn't have to attend meetings on other matters. (No change.)

Exercise 4
1 You shouldn't have been late.
2 They should have answered.
3 You should have sent the letter yesterday.
4 I should have been told.
5 You shouldn't have come.
6 You shouldn't have forgotten your books.
7 He shouldn't have lied.
8 They should have been happy.
9 She shouldn't have behaved so foolishly.
10 You shouldn't have believed him.
11 You should have loved her.
12 The water pipes shouldn't have cracked.

Exercise 5

YOU MUSTN'T ...	YOU DON'T HAVE TO ...
1, 4, 5, 7, 10, 11, 12	2, 3, 6, 8, 9, 13, 14

UNIT 11
Exercise 1
1 e 2 c 3 h 4 m 5 j 6 b 7 k 8 i 9 d 10 a 11 g 12 f 13 l

Exercise 2
1 Do I have to come?
2 Have I got to eat up all my dinner?
3 Have I got to tidy up my room?
4 Do I have to thank Auntie for her present?
5 Do I have to comb my hair?
6 Have I got to take a bath?
7 Do I have to brush my teeth?
8 Do I have to put on my pyjamas?
9 Have I got to meet my cousin?
10 Do I have to let him play with my toys?
11 Have I got to wash my hands?
12 Do I have to help my sister?

Exercise 3
1 Arnold needs to diet, he weighs 100 kilos! Jackie needn't diet, she only weighs 50 kilos. 2 Jackie needs to grow taller, she is only 1.45 metres. Arnold needn't grow taller, he is 1.90 metres. 3 Arnold needs to get a haircut, his hair is long. Jackie needn't get a haircut, her hair is short. 4 Arnold needs to do more exercise, he is unhealthy. Jackie needn't do more exercise, she is healthy. 5 Jackie needs to be more outgoing, she is an introvert. Arnold needn't be more outgoing, he is an extrovert. 6 Jackie needs to be more sociable, she has no friends. Arnold needn't be more sociable, he has many friends. 7 Arnold needs to dress more smartly, he wears old scruffy clothes. Jackie needn't dress more smartly, she wears fashionable clothes. 8 Jackie needs to wear glasses, she is short-sighted. Arnold needn't wear glasses, he has normal vision. 9 Jackie needs to work harder, she is lazy. Arnold needn't work harder, he is hard-working. 10 Arnold needs to take medicine, he is diabetic. Jackie needn't take medicine, she has no illnesses. 11 Jackie needs to study more, her school test score is only 44% Arnold needn't study more, his school test score is 96%. 12 Arnold needs to work for money, he has a part time job. Jackie needn't work for money, her father gives her some.

Exercise 4

OBLIGATION	2, 8, 9
AVOIDABLE OBLIGATION	3
NECESSITY	1, 5
EXEMPTION	4, 6, 10
PROHIBITION	7

UNIT 12
Exercise 1
1 c: can't 2 k: couldn't 3 j: can 4 i: can't 5 l: can / can't 6 h: couldn't 7 g: can't 8 d: can 9 a: could 10 b: can 11 e: couldn't 12 f: can't

Exercise 2
1 You could have gone to the concert.
2 They could have asked me.
3 She could have come.
4 They could have told you.
5 Dennis could have brought his money.
6 Wendy could have made a decision.
7 The police could have arrested Purcell.
8 Philip could have walked her home.
9 They could have reduced the price.
10 You could have bought me a present.
11 He could have said he was innocent.
12 You could have attended the interview.

Exercise 3
1 I couldn't have gone to the concert because I didn't have a ticket.
2 They couldn't have asked you because they never had a chance to speak to you.
3 She couldn't have come because she had another engagement.
4 They couldn't have told me because they haven't seen me for weeks.
5 Dennis couldn't have brought his money because he had lost his wallet, or so he said.
6 Wendy couldn't have made a decision until she was sure of all the facts.
7 The police couldn't have arrested Purcell until they had seen him commit a theft.
8 Philip couldn't have walked her home because he had twisted his ankle.
9 They couldn't have reduced the price because only the manager had the authority to do that.
10 I couldn't have bought you a present as I had no money. Sorry!
11 He couldn't have said he was innocent because he was caught with the stolen watch on his wrist.
12 I couldn't have attended the interview as I got very nervous, started panicking, and fainted.

Exercise 4
Five years ago George was able to have a normal conversation. Now George is able to speak but he is unable to understand other people. In five years time George will be unable to produce words. He will only be able to produce sounds.

Five years ago George was able to cook his own food. Now George is unable to cook his own food, but he is able to feed himself. In five years time George will be unable to feed himself. He will need to be fed.

Five years ago George was able to wash himself. Now George is able to wash himself, but he is unable to get into the bath without help. In five years time George will be unable to wash himself. he will ned washing.
(Some variation possible)

Exercise 5
1 being unable to or not being able to 2 couldn't 3 can't 4 be unable to / not be able 5 couldn't

UNIT 13
Exercise 1
1 can 2 could 3 could 4 can 5 can 6 could 7 could 8 can 9 can 10 could 11 could 12 can

Exercise 2
(Note: It is possible to write positive answers in the negative and negative answers in the positive in this exercise.)

1 He may / might get caught.
2 The weather may / might improve.
3 He may / might not come.
4 My father may / might change his mind.
5 The bank may / might not be open.
6 You may / might succeed.
7 He may / might die.
8 It may / might be broken.
9 He may / might not be English.
10 It may / might (not) be his birthday this week.
11 She may / might (not) agree to an interview.
12 He may / might not answer.

Exercise 3
(Note: as Exercise 2)
1 He may / might have got caught.
2 The weather may / might have improved.
3 He may / might have come.

4 My father may / might have changed his mind.
5 The bank may / might not have been open.
6 You may / might have suceeded.
7 He may / might have died.
8 It may / might have been broken.
9 He may / might not have been English.
10 It may / might (not) have been his birthday this week.
11 She may / might (not) have agreed to an interview.
12 He may / might not have answered.

Exercise 4
1 c 2 g 3 j 4 l 5 a 6 f 7 i 8 d 9 k 10 b 11 h 12 e

Exercise 5

SPEAKER UNCERTAIN	1, 4, 5, 6, 10, 12
SPEAKER HAS KNOWLEDGE	2, 3, 7, 8, 9, 11

1 The speaker does not know if it was Shiela or if it was Sandra.
2 The speaker knows it was not a great party because Dennis ruined it.
3 The speaker knows that it was possible for 'you' to catch the bus if you had missed the train.
4 The speaker does not know whether he/she picked something up by mistake or not.
5 The speaker does not know if 'she' has had her hair dyed from blonde to red or not.
6 The speaker does not know whether 'she' had changed her name or not.
7 The speaker knows that 'you' didn't plan things well, despite being late to.
8 The speaker knows that 'we' didn't organize the event and that the council did.
9 The speaker knows that the meeting is not over even though it was possible to finish an hour earlier.
10 The speaker does not know whether 'he' has lost his way or not.
11 The speaker knows that 'he' did not get the sales job last year.
12 The speaker does not know whether 'we' have won the lottery or not.

Exercise 6
1 He couldn't have been clever.
2 She couldn't have spoken English.
3 He couldn't have drowned.
4 They couldn't have bought a Rolls Royce.
5 I couldn't have made a mistake.
6 He couldn't have joined the choir.
7 He couldn't have gone swimming.
8 She couldn't have replied.
9 He couldn't have been unaware.
10 I couldn't have refused.
11 They couldn't have been friends.
12 He couldn't have helped.

UNIT 14
Exercise 1
1 They should arrive in Brussels on Wednesday evening.
They should leave Brussels on Friday morning.
They should stay in Brussels for two nights.
They should be on the train to Amsterdam on Friday morning.
2 They should arrive in Amsterdam on Friday evening.
They should leave Amsterdam on Sunday morning.
They should stay in Amsterdam for two nights.
They should be on the train to Bonn on Sunday morning.
3 They should arrive in Bonn on Sunday evening.
They should leave Bonn on Monday morning.
They should stay in Bonn for one night.
They should be on motor bikes to Munich on Monday morning.
4 They should arrive in Munich on Monday evening.
They should leave Munich on Thursday morning.
They should stay in Munich for three nights.
They should be on the bus to Vienna on Thursday morning.
5 They should arrive in Vienna on Thursday evening.
They should leave Vienna on Saturday evening.
They should stay in Vienna for two nights.
They should be on the night-coach to Venice on Saturday night.

Exercise 2
1 They ought to have arrived in Venice on Sunday morning.
They ought to have left Venice on Thursday morning.
They ought to have stayed in Venice for four nights.
They ought to have been driving a hire car to Milan on Thursday morning.
2 They ought to have arrived in Milan on Thursday evening.
They ought to have left Milan on Friday morning.
They ought to have stayed in Milan for one night.
They ought to have been on the train to Bern on Friday morning.
3 They ought to have arrived in Bern on Friday evening.
They ought to have left Bern on Saturday evening.
They ought to have stayed in Bern for one night.
They ought to have been on the aeroplane to Paris on Saturday evening.
4 They ought to have arrived in Paris on Saturday evening.
They ought to have left Paris on Sunday morning.
They ought to have stayed in Paris for one night.
They ought to have been on the train to Calais on Sunday morning.

Exercise 3
1 c: shouldn't have gone 2 d: shouldn't have gone 3 d: shouldn't have done 4 c: shouldn't have done 5 a: should have come 6 b: should have come 7 a: should have won 8 b: should have won 9 b: should have returned 10 a: should have returned 11 d: shouldn't have made 12 c: shouldn't have made

Exercise 4
In the future most people will live in very big cities. The countryside will become depopulated as people move to the city looking for work. Many will find jobs but many others won't. The cities will become overcrowded and polluted. Housing will become difficult to find and will become very expensive. Many people won't be able to afford the high city rents. They will be evicted from their homes and join the ever growing influx of people from the countryside living homeless on the streets. Many will become beggars, still more will turn to crime. Others will turn to drugs to escape the pain. They won't gain very much from the new consumer capitalism.

A few people will be rich. The professional and managerial class will do well, but the owners of the large, multi-national companies will comprise the super-rich. They will have country mansions and penthouse apartments in the city. They won't have to worry about the beggars on the streets because they will travel by helicopters.

The rest of us will be left down below, desperately trying to survive. Many of us will not.

UNIT 15
Exercise 1
1 Can I have another of your chocolates? Yes, you can. 2 Could I use your computer? Certainly, go ahead. 3 May I stay up late and watch TV? Yes, you may. 4 Could I have a lift? Yes, of course. 5 Can I hang my picture above the fireplace. Yes, you can. 6 May I sit near the fire? Yes, you may. 7 Could I make myself a sandwich? Certainly, go ahead. 8 Can I borrow your new tie? Yes, you can. 9 May I visit Grandma? Yes, you may. 10 Can I play football on Wednesday afternoon? Yes, you can. 11 Can I go with you? Yes, you can. 12 Could I invite Jayne for dinner on Friday evening? Yes, of course.

Exercise 2
1 c 2 l 3 a 4 j 5 b 6 g 7 d 8 i 9 h 10 k 11 f 12 e

Exercise 3
1 May I be excused? No, you may not 2 Can Lynne go first? No, she can't. 3 Could Gemma have a biscuit? No, she couldn't. 4 May little pussy have some milk? No, he may not. 5 Can I feed the goldfish? No, you can't. 6 Could she just have a minute of your time? No, she couldn't. 7 May I leave the table? No, you may not. 8 Can the dog come into the living room? No, it can't. 9 Could I use your study to work in? No, you couldn't. 10 May we enquire into your whereabouts? No, you may not. 11 Can John and Sylvia come to dinner? No, they may not. 12 Could I let the budgie out of its cage? No, you couldn't. 13 May I use your phone 14 Could I see you again? 15 Can I take my study leave during the Summer term? 16 Could Harold help me with this work? 17 Can we do this exercise in groups instead of individually? or Can we do this exercise individually instead of in groups? 18 May I join you on the boat trip? 19 Could I bring my wife next time? 20 May we borrow your car this evening?

Exercise 4
(Note: the responses 4, 6, 8, 10 & 12 are also interchangeable.)
1 Would you mind if I were excused? No, not at all.
2 Would you mind if Lynne went first? Yes, I would.
3 Would you mind if Gemma had a biscuit? No, of course not.
4 Would you mind if little pussy had some milk? Yes, I would mind.
5 Would you mind if I fed the goldfish? No, not at all.
6 Would you mind if she just had a minute of your time? I'm afraid I would.
7 Would you mind if I left the table? No, of course not.
8 Would you mind if the dog came into the living room? Yes, I would.
9 Would you mind if I used your study to work in? No, not at all.
10 Would you mind if we enquired into your whereabouts? Yes, I would mind.
11 Would you mind if John and Sylvia came to dinner? No, of course not.
12 Would you mind if I let the budgie out of its cage? Yes, I'm afraid I would.

UNIT 16
Exercise 1
1 He used to be a dentist but now he is retired.
2 He used to live in England but now he lives in Australia.
3 He used to be married but now he is divorced.
4 He used to play cricket but now he goes surfing.
5 He used to drink tea or coffee but now he drinks fruit juice.
6 He used to eat fish and chips and roast beef but now he eats seafood and salads.
7 He used to read *The Times* but now he reads *The Australian Outlook*.
8 He used to spend the evening watching TV but now he spends the evening eating in restaurants.
9 He used to weigh 100kgs but now he weighs 70kgs.
10 He used to be unhealthy and fat but now he is healthy and slim.
11 He used to feel sad and stressed but now he feels happy and relaxed.
12 He used to be shy but now he is outgoing.

Exercise 2
1 was 2 would stand 3 looked 4 would say 5 would reply 6 asked 7 announced 8 got 9 smashed 10 gave up 11 retired 12 let

Revision Test 1
1 speak 2 have lived 3 have been cooking 4 had fed 5 has made 6 boils 7 am not doing 8 went 9 come 10 was playing

Questions 11 – 20

FIXED FUTURE	24
FUTURE ARRANGEMENT	29
PREDICTION	23, 28, 30
PROMISE	22
SUGGESTION	27
POLITE ENQUIRY	21
VERY NEAR FUTURE	26
FUTURE ARRANGEMENT (IN THE PAST)	25

21 ✓ 22 ✗ 23 ✗ 24 ✓ Yes:(non) activity in the past becomes refusal. 25 ✓ 26 must 27 can or is able to 28 need to or have to or have got to 29 mustn't 30 can or may or might 31 ought to or should 32 May or could 33 can't 34 needn't or don't need to or don't have to 35 should
36 could or was able to 37 could or might or may 38 had to 39 will 40 be able to

UNIT 17
Exercise 1
1 j 2 a 3 d 4 f 5 h 6 e 7 i 8 k 9 b 10 g 11 l 12 c

Exercise 2
(Note: some variations may be possible in this exercise.)
1 If there had been work, Albert could have stayed in the countryside.
2 If Albert had been skilled, he could have found a well-paid job.
3 If Mary hadn't thought that Albert was ugly, he could have married her.
4 If Albert hadn't broken his leg, he could have been a footballer.
5 If Albert had been able to speak French, he could have moved to France.

6 If Albert had had enough money, he could have started a business.
7 If the bank had liked Albert's business idea, they might have lent him some money.
8 If Albert had been able to swim, he could have got a job as a lifeguard.
9 If Albert hadn't been afraid of heights, he could have been a mountain climber.
10 If Albert hadn't won the lottery and become a millionaire, he would have robbed a bank.

Exercise 3
1 I wouldn't have begun talking to him.
2 I wouldn't have sat down beside him on a park bench.
3 I wouldn't have tried it on.
4 I wouldn't have said I wanted to buy it.
5 I wouldn't have given him my wallet.
6 I wouldn't have returned it to him.
7 I wouldn't have behaved (so stupidly).

Exercise 4
1 If you had studied harder, you could have passed the exam.
2 If my father hadn't been poor, I might have had a decent education.
3 If I had not escaped his influence, I would be dead by now.
4 If he had broken his leg a week earlier, he could not have climbed the wall.
5 If I had arrived sooner, I might have saved her life.
6 If you had lived an honest life, you would not have spent half of it in jail.
7 If a doctor hadn't been present, I might have died.
8 If he had flown to France, he would not have had a ferry ticket in his pocket.
9 If I had gone to the interview, I might have got the job.
10 If you had done as you were told, you would not have got into trouble.
11 If I had decided to get divorced, I would have been deeply unhappy.
12 If he had left before 9.00, he couldn't have answered the phone at 9.30.

Exercise 5

CRITICISM	1, 6, 10
DEDUCTION	4, 8, 12
REGRET / MISSED OPPORTUNITY	2, 5, 9
RELIEF	3, 7, 11

UNIT 18
Exercise 1
1 f: possibility **2** e: suggestion **3** b: suggestion **4** c: possibility or suggestion **5** a: suggestion **6** d: possibility

Exercise 2
(Note: in each case the sentence may be written with the conditional clause first or second.)
1 If you take your medicine, you will get better.
2 You will get rich if you save your money.
3 If the car starts, we will go to London.
4 I will miss my appointment if the bus is late.
5 If you do that, you will cause an accident.
6 You will be punished if you misbehave.
7 If you aren't careful, you will break the vase.
8 I will fly first class if I win the lottery.
9 If he wastes time he will not succeed.
10 She will not take the job if the salary is low.

Exercise 3
1 If you live in the countryside, life is quiet.
2 If you polish silver, it shines.

3 If you go to the theatre on Wednesdays, there is opera.
4 If you eat sweets, they damage your teeth.
5 If you touch marble, it feels cool.
6 If you add salt, it improves the flavour.
7 If you burn incense, it smells sweet.
8 If you take the motorway, there is a lot of traffic.

Exercise 4
1 if she isn't working. **2** If Anna isn't ready, **3** If it's raining, **4** if she is late. **5** if the manager's not there.

Exercise 5

FUTURE CERTAINTY	2, 3, 10, 11
SUGGESTION	1
FACT	5, 9, 13
HABIT	4, 6
RULE	7, 12
POSSIBILITY	8

UNIT 19
Exercise 1
1 e 2 f 3 a 4 d 5 i 6 g 7 c 8 j 9 b 10 l 11 h 12 k

Exercise 2
1 If she won the contest, she'd be happy.
2 If you telephoned him, he'd be shocked.
3 If you ate that, you'd feel sick.
4 If you worked overtime, you'd earn more money.
5 If you stopped talking, we'd hear the radio.
6 If she passed the exams, she'd go to college.
7 If you dieted, you'd lose weight.
8 If you did that, I'd be angry.
Or: If I did that, you'd be angry.
9 If you told her, she'd tell everybody.
10 If you went quietly, they wouldn't be disturbed.
11 If the corner shop were closed, we could shop at the supermarket.
12 If the car broke down, we'd be late.

Exercise 3
Phil: Do you remember music classes with Mr Nightingale?
Kim: The one with the funny face? Oh, yes, I remember him: he had the most awful expressions.
Phil: Yes, <u>if he was playing happy songs, he had a ridiculous smile on his face</u>.
Kim: And <u>if he was playing sad songs, he started to cry</u>.
Phil: Whenever the headmaster came into class, Nightingale would bow!
Kim: And each time the headmaster asked Mr Nightingale a question, he would answer: Yes, sir! Yes, sir! Yes, sir!
Phil: Bowing all the time!
Kim: And wasn't the headmaster awful.
Phil: <u>If you arrived late, he shouted: Report to my office, at break!</u>
Kim: And <u>if you weren't neatly dressed, he sent you home.</u>
Phil: And <u>if you forgot your tie, he'd punish you.</u>
Kim: He was always getting angry with you for forgetting your tie.
Phil: Well, my brother had lost his tie and <u>whenever he could, he took mine, so I was often without one.</u>
Kim: And that explains why <u>whenever the headmaster came into class, you would look down at your book.</u>
Phil: Yes; <u>each time he came in I stared straight down.</u> I was praying that he wouldn't notice my tie was missing!

Kim: Ah, the good old days ...

Exercise 4

If + past + would + verb stem	If + past + verb, past tense
3, 4, 7, 9	1, 2, 5, 6, 8, 10

Exercise 5

FUTURE CERTAINTY	2, 8
POSSIBILITY	7, 10, 12
SUGGESTION	4
FACT	1, 9
PAST HABIT	3, 6, (12)
GENERAL HABIT	5
RULE	11

UNIT 20
Exercise 1
1 d 2 f 3 l 4 k 5 c 6 b 7 j 8 a 9 e 10 h 11 g 12 i

Exercise 2

IF + PAST, WOULD (OR MODAL) + BASE VERB	1, 3, 4, 6, 8
IF + PAST, WOULD (OR MODAL) + PRESENT PERFECT	2, 5, 7, 9, 10, 11, 12

Exercise 3
1 present or future **2** past **3** present **4** present **5** future **6** present **7** past **8** present **9** past **10** future **11** past **12** future

Exercise 4

UNREAL PAST + PAST CONSEQUENCE	1, 12, 13, 15
UNREAL PAST + PRESENT CONSEQUENCE	4
UNREAL PAST + FUTURE CONSEQUENCE	9
IMPOSSIBLE / UNREAL PRESENT	8, 14
IMPOSSIBLE / IMPROBABLE FUTURE	11
DEDUCTION	6
PAST HABIT	2, 10
HABIT	7
FUTURE CERTAINTY	3
FUTURE POSSIBILITY	5

UNIT 21
Exercise 1
1 d 2 j 3 e 4 g 5 b 6 i 7 k 8 c 9 l 10 h 11 f 12 a

Exercise 2
1 We'll have Chinese food if the Indian Restaurant isn't open.
2 I work at home on Thursdays if I don't have a meeting at the office.
3 We play golf every weekend if the course isn't flooded.
3 He sings at the local club if a guest band isn't playing.
4 I will switch the music off if you don't turn down the volume.
5 She doesn't wear make-up if she isn't meeting a boy.
6 They picnic most summer weekends if the weather doesn't prevent them.
7 He won't do a thing if you don't pay him.
8 We'll rent a video if you don't want to go to the cinema.
9 George will give you a lift if his car isn't full.
10 I won't help you if you don't help me.
11 Sheila can do the shopping if she wants to.

Exercise 3
1 (Possible) Unless you hurry, you'll miss the train. **2** (Not possible)
3 (Not possible) **4** (Possible) You won't live beyond sixty, unless you stop smoking. **5** (Possible) Unless you set off before seven, you get caught in the traffic. **6** (not possible) **7** (not possible)
8 (possible) They went sailing every summer, unless they were short of money. **9** (not possible) **10** (possible) We made our own breakfast, unless mother had already done so. **11** (not possible) **12** (possible) He would talk for hours, unless he was feeling ill.

Exercise 4
1 Unless you finish your dinner you can't have any pudding.
If you don't finish your dinner you can't have any pudding.
2 Unless you listen carefully you'll forget.
If you don't listen carefully you'll forget.
3 Unless you chew your food thoroughly you'll get indigestion.
If you don't chew your food thoroughly you'll get indigestion.
4 Unless you wear a suit and tie, they won't let you in.
If you don't wear a suit and tie, they won't let you in.
5 Unless you take the proper equipment, you'll put the expedition in danger.
If you don't take the proper equipment, you'll put the expedition in danger.
6 Unless you answer all the questions you will lose marks.
If you don't answer all the questions you will lose marks.
7 Unless you take care you will hurt yourself.
If you don't take care you will hurt yourself.
8 Unless you believe me, nobody will.
If you don't believe me, nobody will.
9 Unless you behave well, you'll disgrace us.
If you don't behave well, you'll disgrace us.
10 Unless you bring a sandwich, you'll be hungry.
If you don't bring a sandwich, you'll be hungry.
11 Unless you tell the manager, you'll get into trouble.
If you don't tell the manager, you'll get into trouble.
12 Unless you book your hotel in advance, you might not get a room.
If you don't book your hotel in advance, you might not get a room.

Exercise 5
1 Finish your dinner or you can't have any pudding. **2** Listen carefully otherwise you'll forget. **3** Chew your food thoroughly or you'll get indigestion. **4** Wear a suit and tie, otherwise they won't let you in.
5 Take the proper equipment, otherwise you'll put the expedition in danger.
6 Answer all the questions or you will lose marks. **7** Take care or you'll hurt yourself. **8** Believe me, otherwise nobody will. **9** Behave well, or you'll disgrace us. **10** Bring a sandwich, otherwise you'll be hungry. **11** Tell the manager, or you'll get into trouble.
12 Book your hotel in advance, otherwise you might not get a room.

Exercise 6
1 If you are not over 21 years of age
2 Unless you are recommended by another member
3 You must pay a yearly membership fee of £150

4 You should dress smartly
5 You should behave respectfully towards other members
6 If you don't pay for all purchases in cash
7 Vacate club premises by 3.00 a.m.
8 You must sign in all non-member guests
9 Be responsible for guests' actions
10 Unless you obey the rules
11 Follow all additional instructions of the House Manager
12 If you don't know the safety regulations and location of fire exits

UNIT 22
Exercise 1
1 I wish the cat had come home.
2 I wish she had gone to the fair.
3 I wish the government had changed the law.
4 I wish she had fallen in love with me.
5 I wish the sun had shone.
6 I wish he had got a new job.
7 I wish they hadn't closed the local cinema.
8 I wish you had bought a new car.
9 I wish she hadn't brought her husband.
10 I wish they hadn't done that.
11 I wish the children hadn't caused so much trouble.
12 I wish Julie had been my friend.

Exercise 2
1 I wish the cat would come home.
2 I wish she would go / were going to the fair.
3 I wish the government weren't changing the law.
4 I wish she would fall in love with me.
5 I wish the sun would shine.
6 I wish he would get a new job.
7 I wish they weren't closing the local cinema.
8 I wish you would buy a new car.
9 I wish she weren't bringing her husband.
10 I wish Julie would be my friend.

Exercise 3
1 I wish I was called Rosie Rage instead of being called Sarah Smith.
2 I wish I was 18 years old instead of being 15.
3 I wish I had curly red hair instead of having straight brown hair.
4 I wish I was tall instead of being short.
5 I wish I was famous instead of being unknown.
6 I wish I was a pop singer instead of being a singer in the school choir.
7 I wish I lived in my own apartment instead of living with my parents.
8 I wish I drove a sports car instead of riding a bicycle.
9 I wish I had lots of boyfriends instead of not having one.
10 I wish I wore skin-tight leathers instead of wearing a school uniform.
11 I wish I went on holiday abroad instead of going on holiday in Brighton.
12 I wish I earned millions instead of earning £30 a week in my part-time job.

Exercise 4
1 e 2 g 3 h 4 c 5 j 6 f 7 i 8 k 9 b 10 l 11 a 12 d

Exercise 5

WISHES ABOUT THE		
PAST	PRESENT	FUTURE
2, 4, 10, 12	1, 6, 7, 11	3, 5, 8, 9

Exercise 6
1 I wish you did your homework. Then your father would be happy.

2 I wish I were beautiful. Then he would take me out.
3 I wish you would try harder. Then you would do better.
4 wish you would help me next week. Then you would get a reward.
5 I wish I had been you. Then I would have told him what to do with his money.
6 I wish they would make up their minds. Then I would be able to plan my schedule.
7 I wish you didn't smoke. Then you wouldn't have bad breath.
8 I wish you would go to school. Then you wouldn't get into trouble.
9 I wish he hadn't lost his money. Then we could have gone out for dinner.
10 I wish she would telephone. Then I wouldn't be worried.
11 I wish you wouldn't ignore me. Then I wouldn't cry.
12 I wish you would answer my questions. Then I wouldn't have to tell the police.
13 I wish he'd hear soon. Then he won't get depressed.
14 I wish you'd travel across Europe by car. Then I'd come with you.
15 I wish Peter would come. Then I shouldn't have to cancel the meeting.
16 I wish I'd bought that computer. Then I could have done this in half the time.
17 I wish he'd told me there was a problem. Then I could have helped him.
18 I wish they'd get the contract. Then we wouldn't lose our jobs.
19 I wish he hadn't bought that painting. Then we could have gone to Australia for our holiday.
20 I wish you'd give me some encouragement. Then I'd go in for the exam.

UNIT 23
Exercise 1
1 She said that he was looking for a pencil.
2 She said that she had answered enough questions already.
3 She said that she had been thinking about it since the day before.
4 She said that I had earned a lot of money in the previous year.
5 She said that they had been going to the fair when it had started raining.

Exercise 2
1 She told me that she would discuss it with Paul the following day.
2 She told me that he might have been there the previous night.
3 She told me that she could meet me at nine-o'clock.
4 She told me that they hadn't left her without any help.
5 She told me that she had been sick for two weeks before Christmas.

Exercise 3
1 He claimed that he didn't know her.
2 She insisted that I go with her.
3 I reassured him/her that she wasn't stupid.
4 The Professor explained that there was a solution to every problem.
5 The Leader of The Opposition argued that the government had been foolish to make such a decision.
6 I decided that I would attend the meeting.
7 I thought that you were in charge.
8 He assured me that I would not lose my benefit.
9 They felt that they had been abandoned.
10 The Prime Minister informed the press that war was expected.

Exercise 4
1 I will be visiting Ireland as soon as I can.
2 I am too busy.
3 I am not responsible.
4 It has been a terrible experience.
5 I didn't discover the cause of the illness quickly enough to save your baby.
6 I'll have a cheeseburger and fries.
7 You were an efficient employee.
8 You are right.
9 You will be sorry.
10 You have lied in the past.
11 Don't say anything until the problem has been solved.
12 Shall I come with you?

Exercise 5
1 d 2 g 3 a 4 e 5 h 6 b 7 f 8 c

UNIT 24
1 What's your 2 How ... are you 3 Where do you ... from 4 Where do you live 5 Have you 6 Are you 7 you have 8 What do you 9 what do you 10 do you speak 11 What do you 12 What is

Exercise 2
1 what her name was 2 how old she was 3 where she came from 4 where she lived in Japan 5 if she had ever been outside Japan 6 if she was married 7 if she had any children 8 what she did 9 what she studied 10 which languages she spoke 11 what she liked doing in her spare time 12 what her ambition was

Exercise 3
1 Tom told Edward to look out.
2 Dianne told Anna not to leave.
3 He told her to think before she acted.
4 The sergeant told the soldiers to stand to attention.
5 Joan told Anne to bring her a biscuit.
6 Judith told Tony to be careful or he'd hurt himself.
7 Nicky told Joan not to speak with her mouth full.
8 Helen told Alan to turn off the lights when he went.
9 Jane told Terry and Tony to enjoy themselves.
10 The manager told his secretary to call him a taxi.
11 Nelson told John to shut up.
12 John told Nelson to put down the gun.
13 Tim told Margaret to give him the money.
14 Margaret told Tim not to shoot her.
15 The teacher told the students not to start writing until he gave them permission.

Exercise 4
1 Colonel Sanders demanded that they improve their performance.
2 Colonel Sanders instructed them to polish their boots.
3 Colonel Sanders reminded them not to forget their duty.
4 Colonel Sanders commanded them to attack.
5 Colonel Sanders insisted that they did not retreat.
6 Colonel Sanders warned them that cowards would be shot.
7 Colonel Sanders directed them to go to their positions.
8 Colonel Sanders urged them not to give in.
9 Colonel Sanders asked them to remember who they were.
10 Colonel Sanders implored them to fight like heroes and posterity would remember them.
11 Colonel Sanders begged them not to abandon their posts.
12 Colonel Sanders told them that soldiers who had not fought hard would have to assist him cooking his

special chicken dinner for the troops who had.

Exercise 5
1 help me you help me, please 2 you do the washing up, please; do the washing up 3 you turn on the television, please; turn on the television 4 don't forget about me 5 you post this letter, please; post this letter 6 you bring me a newspaper, please; bring me a newspaper 7 don't go 8 marry me; you marry me

UNIT 25
1 doing 2 losing 3 to look 4 to say 5 to hurt 6 going 7 hitting 8 kissing 9 studying or to study 10 winning

Exercise 2
1 b 2 a & b 3 b 4 b 5 a 6 a 7 a 8 a

Exercise 3
1 to take 2 taking 3 to get 4 writing 5 to buy 6 to do 7 to do 8 being 9 to think 10 having 11 thinking 12 trying

Exercise 4
1 to inform 2 to result 3 to refuse 4 to take 5 drinking 6 burning or to burn 7 asking 8 to give 9 returning 10 watching 11 doing 12 laughing or to laugh 13 laughing or to laugh 14 dancing 15 singing 18 to hear 19 to receive

UNIT 26
Exercise 1
1 ringing 2 to get 3 to open 4 using 5 to find 6 to imagine 7 looking 8 to lift 9 banging 10 to fix 11 to repair 12 to hold 13 to kill 14 to do 15 flying

Exercise 2
1 to wear 2 bathing 3 to enter 4 visiting 5 to eat 6 to bring 7 to talk 8 to play 9 to touch 10 attempting 11 staying 12 walking

Exercise 3
1 Wearing protective clothing is advised.
2 Bathing in designated areas is allowed.
3 Entering without a member's card is not permitted.
4 Visiting during mealtimes is forbidden.
5 Eating your own food on restaurant premises is not allowed.
6 Bringing a packed lunch is advised.
7 Talking during exams is not permitted.
8 Playing music on the Underground is forbidden.
9 Touching the items on display is allowed.
10 Attempting the climb by yourself is not advised.
11 Staying out late is not permitted.
12 Walking outside the Public Access areas is not allowed.

Exercise 4
1 to go ; travelling or to travel ; to spend
2 going or to go ; to go ; going or to go
3 watching ; playing ; to have ; to have played

UNIT 27
Exercise 1
1 Tony would prefer to go rowing.
2 Tony would prefer to play football.
3 Tony would prefer to do judo.
4 Tony would prefer to go rock-climbing.
5 Tony would prefer to play tennis.
6 Tony would prefer to go fishing.
7 Tony would prefer to play badminton.
8 Tony would prefer to go white-water rafting.
9 Tony would rather do karate.
10 Tony would rather play rugby.
11 Tony would rather go hang-gliding.
12 Tony would rather play cricket.

Exercise 2
1 Wouldn't you sooner go cycling?
2 Wouldn't you rather play golf?
3 Wouldn't you prefer to do fencing?

4 Wouldn't you sooner go canoeing?
5 Wouldn't you rather play squash
6 Wouldn't you prefer to go swimming?
7 Wouldn't you sooner play hockey?
8 Wouldn't you prefer to go hiking?
9 Wouldn't you sooner do archery?
10 Wouldn't you sooner play rounders?
11 Wouldn't you prefer to go mountaineering?
12 Wouldn't you rather do kendo?

Exercise 3
1 would prefer 2 prefer 3 would rather 4 prefer 5 would rather 6 would rather 7 would prefer 8 would rather 9 prefer 10 would rather 11 would prefer 12 prefer

UNIT 28
Exercise 1
1 rose 2 were being made 3 were shocked 4 had happened 5 had come 6 had been provided 7 had been warned 8 approached 9 fel 10 be seen 11 struck 12 be forgotten

Exercise 2
1 are picked 2 are extracted 3 (are) cleaned 4 (are) dried 5 is removed. 6 are sorted 7 (are) graded 8 (are) shipped to world markets 9 are roasted 10 (are) cooled 11 (are) ground 12 being sold to the consumer

Revision Test 2
1 d 2 c 3 b 4 f 5 g 6 h 7 i 8 e 9 j 10 a

GENERAL HABIT	10
EXCEPTION	1, 5
FUTURE POSSIBILITY	4
IMPOSSIBLE / UNREAL PRESENT	3, 6, 8, 9
UNREAL PAST	2, 7

11 I wish I was in Chicago.
12 I wish we were having a New Year's celebration.
or I wish we could have a New Year's celebration.
13 I wish he had been richer.
14 I wish we were going to Australia.
or I wish we could go to Australia.
15 I wish they had come.
16 She told me that she didn't love him.
17 He said that she had been working very hard yesterday.
18 He asked me if I was going to the office party next week.
19 The new manager wondered what my name was.
20 She assured me that I could do it today.
21 Would you like to dance?
22 Please help me! or Will you help me?
23 Marry my daughter!
24 I can do as I like.
25 Don't forget our arrangement.
26 to do 27 to kill 28 Taking 29 eating and to eat 30 meeting 31 prefer 32 would rather 33 would prefer 34 would prefer 35 would rather
36 *Wuthering Heights* was written by Emily Bronte.
37 A lot of money was made by the company in the stock market..
38 The report hasn't been completed.
39 The rubbish had already been removed (by the workmen).
40 The key couldn't be found anywhere.

UNIT 29
Exercise 1
1 A 2 (ø) People 3 The 4 An 5 (ø) Butterflies 6 The 7 (ø) Elephants 8 The 9 The 10 (ø) Water 11 The 12 A

Exercise 2
1 an 2 the 3 the 4 the 5 a or the 6 the 7 the 8 the 9 a 10 the 11 a 12 a

Exercise 3
1 such 2 such a 3 such 4 such a 5 such an 6 such

Exercise 4
1 quite a 2 quite 3 quite 4 quite a 5 quite 6 quite a 7 quite 8 quite

Exercise 5
1 What a 2 Wha 3 What an 4 What 5 What 6 What a 7 What

Exercise 6
1 an 2 (ø) 3 the 4 (ø) 5 the 6 the 7 a 8 (ø) 9 the 10 a 11 (ø) 12 the 13 the 14 the 15 a 16 a 17 the 18 the 19 (ø) 20 the

UNIT 30
Exercise 1
1 much 2 many 3 many 4 a lot of 5 many 6 much 7 much 8 a lot of 9 many 10 much 11 much 12 many

Exercise 2
1 f 2 c 3 e 4 a 5 l 6 j 7 i 8 b 9 d 10 h 11 g 12 k

Exercise 3
1 very many 3 much 4 very 5 very 6 much 7 many 8 very 9 much 10 very 11 many 12 very

Exercise 4
1 much too 2 too much 3 much too 4 too many 5 much too 6 much too 7 too much 8 too many 9 much too 10 too many 11 much too 12 too much

Exercise 5
1 Well done. I'm very satisfied with your results.
2 They are very interesting people.
3 There are many interesting people at the party.
4 Have you made much progress?
5 Hello! I'm very happy to see you.
6 Look at the time. It's very late.
7 Is there much to say?
8 How much English do you speak?
9 How many English are there?
10 Andrew is too tired to do any more work.
11 Have you come back with many good impressions of the places you visited?
or: Have you come back with very good impressions of the places you visited?
12 I am too upset to talk about it.

UNIT 31
Exercise 1
1 We sold few carrots last year.
2 We sold little cheese last year.
3 We sold a lot of eggs last year.
4 We sold little honey last year.
5 We sold little jam last year.
6 We sold little marmalade last year.
7 We sold little meat last year.
8 We sold a lot of milk last year.
9 We sold few onions last year.
10 We sold few oranges last year.
11 We sold a lot of potatoes last year.
12 We sold few tomatoes last year.

Exercise 2
1 much; We have little space.
2 many; The President has got few reliable advisors.
3 many; There are few exciting things to do here.
4 much; There was little pie for pudding.
5 many; I know few rich people.
6 many; The general was informed on few occasions.
7 much; There has been little enthusiasm for my ideas.
8 much; I have got little comfort.
9 many; There have been few changes in recent years.
10 much; There is little activity in the winter.

Exercise 3
1 a little 2 a few 3 a few 4 a little 5 a little 6 a few 7 a few 8 a little 9 a little 10 a few

Exercise 4
1 few 2 a few 3 little 4 a little 5 a little 6 little 7 a few 8 few 9 A few 10 Few 11 little 12 a little

1 c 2 d 3 a 4 f 5 e 6 i 7 b 8 j 9 h 10 g

UNIT 32
Exercise 1
1 two, second 2 three, third 3 four, fourth 4 five, fifth 5 eight, eighth 6 nine, ninth 7 twelve, twelfth 8 fifteen, fifteenth 9 nineteen, nineteenth 10 twenty, twentieth 11 twenty-two, twenty-second 12 fifty-three, fifty-third 13 ninety-one, ninety-first 14 a/one hundred, a/one hundredth 15 a/one thousand, a/one thousandth 16 a/one million, a/one millionth

Exercise 2
1 2nd 2 3rd 3 4th 4 5th 5 8th 6 9th 7 12th 8 15th 9 19th 10 20th 11 22nd 12 53rd 13 91st 14 100th 15 1000th 16 1,000,000th

Exercise 3
1 three hundred and sixty-five 2 five hundred and one 3 seven hundred 4 two thousand 5 four thousand, six hundred and twenty-one 6 five thousand and thirty-four 7 nine thousand and four 8 ten thousand 9 ten thousand and one 10 fourteen thousand, three hundred and forty-two 11 twenty-three thousand and seven 12 forty-five thousand and thirty-four 13 ninety-seven thousand, two hundred 14 ninety-nine thousand, nine hundred and ninety-nine 15 one hundred thousand and five 16 one hundred and forty thousand and fifty-six 17 two hundred and ninety-eight thousand, four hundred and eighty-five 18 one million and seven 19 forty-five million, five hundred and sixty-seven thousand, four hundred and forty-one 20 one hundred million

Exercise 4
1 four-five-six-zero-two 2 seven-six-eight-four-zero-eight 3 six-zero-seven-zero-seven-one 4 six-zero-eight-nine-zero-four 5 six-double zero-seven-eight-one 6 double seven-double one-double four

Exercise 5
1 ten sixty-six 2 fourteen ninety-four 3 seventeen eighty-nine 4 eighteen forty-eight 5 nineteen sixteen 6 two thousand

Exercise 6
1 the twenty-eighth of February; February the twenty-eighth
2 the fourth of March; March the fourth
3 the fifteenth of May; May the fifteenth
4 the twenty-second of June; June the twenty-second
5 the twenty-first of July, nineteen sixty-four; July the twenty-first, nineteen sixty-four
6 the tenth of September, nineteen ninety-nine; September the tenth, nineteen ninety-nine

Exercise 7
1 There are two big elephants in the garden.
2 There are twelve jurors in a jury.
3 Which three people do you mean?
4 It was the second horse in the race.
5 The first three runners receive a medal.
6 He was the first one in his family to go to university.

UNIT 33
Exercise 1
1 It's her pen. 2 They're his books. 3 It's their dog. 4 It's my computer. 5 It's your essay. 6 It's his idea. 7 It's their holiday. 8 They're our children. 9 It's their football. 10 It's our environment. 11 It's its habitat. 12 They're its wheels.

Exercise 2
1 Has he put on his shoes?
2 Have you burnt your finger?
3 Have we packed our suitcases?
4 Have they washed their hands?

5 Have I taken my medicine?
6 Has the dog had its walk?

Exercise 3
1 Yes, but you haven't put on yours.
2 Yes, but he hasn't burnt his.
3 Yes, but they haven't packed theirs.
4 Yes, but I haven't washed mine.
5 Yes, but she hasn't taken hers.
6 Yes, but we haven't had ours.

Exercise 4
1 Any winner can bring their ticket here to get their prize.
2 All guests must sign their names in the register.
3 Every member is obliged to pay his or her club fee before next week.
4 Any person not displaying his or her member's card will be refused entry.
5 Each child should bring their own packed lunch.
6 All officers are responsible for cleaning their own uniforms.

Exercise 5
1 His ... hers 2 Her ... his 3 Her ... his 4 Their car ... ours 5 Our car ... theirs 6 Our car ... theirs

UNIT 34
Exercise 1
1 People used to work harder in the past.
2 The cheetah sprinted rapidly across the Savannah
3 I will go by plane to France next year.
4 He looked longingly towards the village.
5 He acts aggressively on the pitch.
6 We enjoyed the movie enormously yesterday.
7 They didn't play very well this morning.
8 He drank his water sparingly in the desert.
9 Children don't behave respectfully nowadays.
10 She flew across the Atlantic last year.
11 The nights come quickly in the North.
12 I whispered softly in her ear.

Exercise 2

| | ADVERBIALS | | |
	MANNER	PLACE	TIME
1	harder*	at her house	on Saturday in the past
2	rapidly	across the Savannah	
3	by plane	to France	next year
4	longingly	towards the village	
5	aggressively	on the pitch	
6	enormously		yesterday
7	very well		this morning
8	sparingly	in the desert	
9	respectfully		nowadays
10		across the Atlantic	last year
11	quickly	in the North	
12	softly	in her ear	

*comparative

Exercise 3
1 YES 2 YES 3 NO 4 NO 5 YES 6 YES 7 YES 8 YES 9 NO 10 YES 11 NO 12 NO

Exercise 4
1 Next year I will be in Rio.
2 Many times I have asked, but I haven't received a reply.
3 In Surrey Street you will find one.
4 Clearly I described the situation.
5 As soon as possible we will get them there.
6 For over an hour I have been standing in the cold.
7 On July 21st I will be flying out of Heathrow Airport.

8 Just after my husband died in 1996 I was there.
9 Tomorrow we are having her over.
10 In the Town Hall they will be able to answer your questions.
11 On Thursday night we can meet.
12 Little by little I persuaded him.

Exercise 5
1 I will be in Rio next year.
2 I have asked many times, but I haven't received a reply.
3 You will find one in Surrey Street.
4 I described the situation clearly.
5 We will get them there as soon as possible.
6 I have been standing in the cold for over an hour.
7 I will be flying out of Heathrow Airport on July 21st.
8 I was there in 1996, just after my husband died.
9 We are having her over tomorrow.
10 They will be able to answer your questions in the Town Hall.
11 We can meet on Thursday night.
12 I persuaded him little by little.

Exercise 6
Vicky was terrified. Slowly[e] and cautiously she opened the door. Her hands were shaking and she was feeling panicky[n]. She glanced nervously[e] up and down the street. Everything was quiet. Faintly echoing[e] in the distance she could hear a train. But the sound faded slowly and disappeared. She could stay no longer. Into the[e] street she stepped, the click-clack of her shoes loudly[e] booming from the pavement[n], echoing in her ears like gun fire. Very[e] quickly she bent down and took off her shoes. She feared the sound. She continued on her way barefoot, her feet moving painfully[n] upon the pavement. Suddenly she saw him. She froze in horror, her worst fear realized. Had he seen her? She dived into an[e] alley and pressed herself into the[n] shadow of a doorway. She was breathing heavily[n]. She held her breath to stifle the sound, but only heard her heart pounding violently[n] in her chest. Faster and faster[e] it beat, louder and louder[n] it pounded. Could she not just stop the fear and die right now[e]? But then she heard something that tore her heart in two. A slow[n], steady, step coming nearer by the second. She let out a terrifying scream, more like a wolf's howl than the cry of a human. Immediately he was on top of her.

'Are these your shoes, Madam?' asked the policeman. 'Be careful or you'll catch cold'.

UNIT 35
Exercise 1
1 A beautiful, big house. 2 A terrible, pink hat. 3 An stylish, leather suit. 4 A impressive, oval stadium. 5 A silly, circular bed. 6 A lovely, little kitten. 7 A shy, middle-aged man. 8 A difficult, English exercise. 9 A comfortable, wooden chair. 10 A dirty, blue shirt. 11 A famous, old woman. 12 A fascinating, new thriller.

Exercise 2

SIZE	SHAPE	AGE
big	oval	middle-aged
little	triangular	old
		new

COLOUR	NATIONALITY	MATERIAL
pink	French	leather
blue	English	wooden

Exercise 3
1 The sea was cold, dark and deep.
2 The moon looked bright and silvery.
3 He was tall, fair and handsome.
4 She looked old and tired.
5 The children were thin, ragged and starving. 6 The stars were clear and distant. 7 The sun was red, orange and yellow. 8 The heat was intense and exhausting. 9 The man seemed polite and friendly. 10 I felt cold, wet and hungry. 11 The Arctic was enormous, silent and empty. 12 The evening was warm, dark and scented with flowers.

Revision Test 3
1 a 2 a 3 a 4 the 5 a 6 (ø) 7 a 8 the 9 the 10 a 11 the 12 the 13 the or (ø) 14 the 15 a or the 16 the 17 an 18 (ø) 19 the 20 a 21 very 22 much 23 many 24 too 25 very 26 little 27 a few 28 few 29 A little 30 a few 31 three hundred and sixty-five 32 one million, one hundred thousand 33 six-oh-seven-oh-seven-one 34 nineteen forty-five 35 the twenty-first of July, nineteen sixty-four 36 my 37 yours 38 Hers 39 Its 40 ours or July the twenty-first, nineteen sixty-four 41 We enjoyed ourselves yesterday. 42 He did his work unwillingly. 43 We are going to a concert in the Town Hall on Saturday. 44 The monkeys were playing noisily in the trees. 45 They were dancing wildly in the square last night. 46 She had big brown eyes. 47 It was a dirty yellow book. 48 She loved old black and white movies. 49 The museum contained some remarkable ancient Greek statues. 50 I put on my stylish new wool jumper.

UNIT 36
Exercise 1
1 ND 2 D 3 ND 4 D 5 D 6 ND 7 D 8 ND 9 D 10 ND 11 D 12 ND

Exercise 2
1 subject 2 subject 3 object 4 subject 5 object 6 subject 7 object 8 object 9 object 10 object 11 subject 12 subject

Exercise 3
1 that departs at 12.30 2 that I gave you 3 that he borrowed from the library 4 that has opened in town 5 that had told a lie 6 that Marlene is on 7 that crashed into Miss Hunter 8 that she watched last week 9 that I / you passed the information to 10 that broke the window 11 that lit the bonfire 12 that Mrs Bates / your wife stabbed you with

Exercise 4
1 We're too late to catch the plane which departs at 12.30. 2 Where is the key which I gave you? Where is the key I gave you? 3 He has returned the book which he borrowed from the library. He has returned the book he borrowed from the library. 4 Are you going to the fair which has opened in town? 5 The press attacked the politician who had told a lie. 6 Is that the bus which Marlene is on? Is that the bus Marlene is on? 7 Who was driving the car which crashed into Miss Hunter? 8 She didn't like the film which she watched last week. She didn't like the film she watched last week. 9 Was the man who you passed the information to a member of MI5? Was the man you passed the information to a member of MI5?
10 The children who broke the window had been playing football.
11 Who was the boy who lit the bonfire?
12 Mr Bates. Is this the knife which your wife stabbed you with? Mr Bates. Is this the knife your wife stabbed you with?

UNIT 37
Exercise 1
1 The boy chosen for the team must be 190 cm tall. 2 The maid given the blankets took them upstairs. 3 The picnickers, sitting in the open, ran for the cover of the trees when it started raining. 4 The lady telling the story was Mrs Carruthers. 5 The book lying on my desk was very valuable. 6 The cake awarded the prize will have to be wonderful. 7 The discovery, made by two passing tourists, will lead to a lot of scientific discussion. 8 I saw an old man dancing in the street! 9 General Smithers, replaced as Commander of the Armed Forces, talked to me earlier about his removal. 10 The infected meat, bought from Billy the Butcher of Birmingham the unsuspecting member of the public, caused food poisoning in the local community. 11 The victims, freed from the wreckage by rescue workers, will be taken to local hospitals. 12 Young men and women, hoping to make it in Hollywood, often end up homeless on the streets of L.A.

Exercise 2
1 passive 2 passive 3 active 4 active 5 active 6 passive 7 passive 8 active 9 passive 10 passive 11 passive 12 active

Exercise 3
Once upon a time, there was a little girl who lived in a forest. Her name was Little Red Riding Hood. She wore a beautiful red cloak with a pretty red hood, which had been made by her mother. One day Little Red Riding Hood was going to visit her grandmother. Mother gave her a basket which was filled with chocolates to take to Grandma.
Be careful of the wolf! said Mother, who was always thinking of her daughter's safety.
'Don't worry,' said Little Red Riding Hood, who was already walking away, 'I'll be fine.'
The wolf, who had been hiding in the bushes, watching and listening in the distance, turned and ran into the forest.
Grandma, who was looking forward to seeing her little granddaughter, was baking some buns for Little Red Riding Hood's arrival. Suddenly, she heard a knock at the door.
'Oh,' she exclaimed, 'that must be her.'
The wolf, who was standing outside, gave Grandma a terrible shock when she opened the door. He picked her up by the ears and locked her in the broom cupboard. Having got rid of Grandma, the wolf went into the bedroom. It was there he noticed Grandma's night-clothes which were scattered on the bed. He put on the nightgown and cap and got into bed. He lay back, laughing to himself, until he heard the sound of footsteps, which was coming from outside.
Little Red Riding Hood knocked, entered and walked into the bedroom.
'Grandma!' she exclaimed, 'What big eyes you've got ...' and to cut a long story short the wolf would have eaten her if a woodcutter, who had been working nearby, hadn't heard her screaming. He ran into the cottage where he chopped off the head of the wolf with an axe he was carrying, which was normally used for cutting wood.
And they all lived happily ever after ...
1 Once upon a time, there was a little girl living in a forest.
2 She wore a beautiful red cloak with a pretty red hood, made by her mother.
3 Mother gave her a basket filled with chocolates to take to Grandma.
4 'Be careful of the wolf!' said Mother, always thinking of her daughter's safety.
5 'Don't worry,' said Little Red Riding Hood, already walking away, 'I'll be fine.'
6 The wolf, hiding in the bushes, watching and listening in the distance, turned and ran into the forest.
7 Grandma, looking forward to seeing her little granddaughter, was baking some buns for Little Red Riding Hood's arrival.
8 The wolf, standing outside, gave Grandma a terrible shock when she opened the door.
9 It was there he noticed Grandma's night-clothes scattered on the bed.
10 He lay back, laughing to himself, until he heard the sound of footsteps, coming from outside.
11 ... a woodcutter, working nearby ...
12 ... with an axe he was carrying, normally used for cutting wood.

Exercise 4
1 DRESSED = passive 2 KNOWN = passive 3 HANGING = active 4 SITTING = active 5 COVERED = passive 6 SMILING = active 7 FAMED = passive 8 TAKEN = passive 9 RISING = active 10 SCATTERED = passive 11 LIVING = active

UNIT 38
Exercise 1
1 That the film has finished is a great relief.
2 I wonder what I should do.
3 I don't know why I said that.
4 How you laughed affected me strongly.
5 I think that fresh food is better than frozen food.
6 That the weather had improved was most welcome.
7 What to do was the question they were all asking.
8 His doubt was whether I would finish on time.
9 Your story is that you went there alone.
10 Why you left was something I couldn't understand.
11 I hope that the game will start soon.
12 Murphy's Law is that if things can go wrong they will.
13 I believe that the time has come.
14 His belief is that flowers grow quicker if you talk to them.

Exercise 2
1 subject 2 object 3 object 4 subject 5 object 6 subject 7 subject 8 compliment 9 compliment 10 subject 11 object 12 compliment 13 object 14 compliment

Exercise 3
1 That the audience were bored upset the actors a lot.
2 Where the money was hidden was a secret.
3 She knows that she is the cleverest student in the class.
4 That the product didn't sell meant the company lost money.
5 The problem was how to climb down without ropes.
6 I realized that I was taking a risk.
7 His belief is that he will see her again.
8 That they were killed was due to bad luck.

9 I don't know why the brakes failed.
10 The question was where to go.
11 What the police announced surprised everybody.
12 What he suggested was a great idea.
Exercise 4
1 He hoped that things would get better soon. (object) His hope was that things would get better soon. (compliment)
2 You could see that the place was in a poor condition. (object) You could see what a poor condition the place was in. (object) **3** I was annoyed that he had taken the car. (object) That he had taken the car annoyed me. (object)
4 The important news is that the Prime Minister has died. (compliment)
That the Prime Minister has died is important news. (object)
5 That there is still a difficulty is appreciated. (subject) It is appreciated that there is still a difficulty. (object)
6 The terrible shock was that the money was gone. (compliment) That the money was gone was a terrible shock. (subject)
7 The information we had been given was that help was coming soon. (compliment) That help was coming soon was the information we had been given. (subject) **8** They discussed something that has aroused my interest. (object) What they discussed aroused my interest. (subject)
Exercise 5
What is love is a question that everybody has asked at some stage in their life. Poets have sung about it, and some romantic people have died for it. *That it concerns us all* is indisputable.
It is a question *that everyone asks and nobody answers*. We ask our parents *how they fell in love* and they usually don't know *what to say*. Do you need to know *when you are in love*? Or is it just necessary to feel *that you are in love*? But is *being in love* the same as love?
That most mothers love their children is commonly accepted; but we are not likely to say *that they are 'in love' with their children*. That the majority of people who get married love each other is also true, but here we would say *that the man and the woman are 'in love' with each other*. Therefore, you could argue *that there are different types of love*.
Can we claim *that love is just a human phenomenon*? Hardly. Animals show *love for their young* in the same way that humans do. We say *that pets – cats and dogs – love their owners*. But is that love or just sense of security? Perhaps that's *what love is – providing and giving a sense of security*.
UNIT 39
Exercise 1
1 d 2 e 3 f 4 a 5 b 6 g 7 h 8 e

Exercise 2
1 therefore **2** therefore **3** Nevertheless **4** therefore **5** nevertheless **6** therefore
Exercise 3
1 a & **1 2** b & q **3** c & g **4** d & i **5** e & p **6** f & o **7** h & k **8** j & r **9** m & n
Exercise 4
1 I was away in Rome when the murder took place. Therefore, I couldn't have been the killer.
2 Animals have the capacity to feel, to think and to communicate, in ways not very different from our own. Therefore they should be treated with respect.
3 My mother had a bad leg. Therefore she needed help to climb the stairs.
4 You talk about your father's brother.

Therefore you are talking about your uncle. **5** He put too much pressure on the strings. Therefore they broke.
6 He had lots of money. Therefore I married him. **7** Most of the ways we see the world are through audio-visual media. Therefore you need to understand the media if you are to understand the world and even yourself. **8** In a relationship, women – not men – have the responsibility and physical burden of giving birth to a child. Therefore women should be given maternity benefit to remedy this inequality and its consequences in the workplace. **9** The money wasn't good enough. Therefore I refused the job offer.
Exercise 5
1 a = therefore   b = however **2** a = therefore   b = however **3** a = therefore   b = however **4** a = therefore   b = therefore **5** a = therefore   b = however

UNIT 40
Exercise 1
1 g 2 c 3 f 4 i 5 d 6 e 7 j 8 h 9 b 10 a
Exercise 2
1 You should eat vegetables because they are good for your health.   **2** As I don't have much money, I bought the cheapest one.   **3** Since they charge less interest, I bank with Natland.   **4** I went out with him because I like him.
5 As the roads were busy, Edward was late for work.   **6** The phone isn't working because I dropped the receiver.   **7** Since fans were fighting with police, the match was cancelled.   **8** You shouldn't go out tonight because I want you to stay in with me.   **9** Spike went to Film School because he wanted to be a movie maker.
10 She left him because he was cruel.
Exercise 3
1 Why should I eat vegetables?
Because they are good for you.
2 Why did you buy the cheapest one?
Because I don't have much money.
3 Why do you bank with Natland? because their services are cheaper.
4 Why did you go out with him?
Because I like him.
5 Why was Edward late to work?
Because the roads were busy.
6 Why isn't the phone working?
Because the aerial has blown down.
Why was the match cancelled?
Because fans were fighting with police.
8 Why shouldn't I go out tonight?
Because I want you to stay in with me.
9 Why did Spike go to Film School?
Because he wanted to be a movie maker.
10 Why did she leave him?
Because he was cruel.
Exercise 4
1 (a) On the way to the interview he straightened his tie) as = time conjunction)
(b) He straightened his tie quickly as he was in a hurry to get to the interview. (as = reason conjunction)
2 (a) During the time I was reading the book I put on my glasses. (as = time conjunction)
(b) I put on my glasses because I needed them to help read the book. (as = reason conjunction)
3 (a) During the period of time that she was watching television her mind was empty. (as = time conjunction)
(b) Her mind was empty because she was watching television and not thinking about anything iin particular. (as = reason conjunction)
4 (a) At the time he was inspecting a species of rare butterfly he picked up

a magnifying glass. (as = time conjunction)
(b) He picked up the magnifying glass because he wanted a better view of the rare species of butterfly he was inspecting. (as = reason conjunction)
5 (a) At the moment she was leaving the house she took the key from her pocket. (as = time conjunction)
(b) She took the key from her pocket because she was leaving the house (and presumably wanted to lock the door). (as = reason conjunction)
Exercise 5
1 time **2** reason **3** reason **4** time **5** time or reason
Exercise 6
1 (a) He didn't leave early [fact] because he was hungry [reason].
(b) He did leave early [fact] not because he was hungry, but for some other reason [reason, not given]).
2 (a) I haven't worked hard during my life [fact] because I'm naturally lazy. [reason]
(b) I have worked hard all my life [fact] not because it's natural to work hard, but for some other reason. [reason (not given)]
3 (a) The children are not allowed to go there [fact] because their mother says they cannot. [reason].
(b) The children are allowed to go there [fact] not because their mother says they can't, but for some other reason. [reason (not given)].
(a) seems more likely. (b) does not make sense except in a very particular circumstance, where perhaps the father looks after the children and allows them to do things the mother does not allow them to do.
4 (a) The movie made little money [fact] because it was a bad movie. [reason].
(b) The movie made a lot of money [fact] not because it was a poor movie but for some other reason [reason (not given)]
(a) seems more likely. (b) does not make sense unless the speaker is being sarcastic.

UNIT 41
Exercise 1
1 c 2 d 3 e 4 b 5 f 6 a
Exercise 2
1 He was such an evil man that everybody hated him – even his own mother. **2** His evil deeds were such that everybody hated him – even his own mother. **3** She was such a beautiful woman that men would fight to be by her side. **4** Her beauty was such that men would fight to be by her side. **5** The cockerel made such a noise that I wanted to throw something at it. **6** The noise of the cockerel was such that I wanted to throw something at it.
Exercise 3
1 so **2** such **3** such **4** so **5** such
Revision Test 4
1 which **2** who **3** who **4** which **5** where **6** that the boys played **7** that is opening today **8** that Sammy found
9 The man carrying those papers is to give a talk. **10** The girl asked to hand over the flowers will be very proud.
11 Dr Foster, known to be a radical, will attend the conference. **12** That the children were noisy upset the teacher.
13 I'm not sure why the car broke down.
14 He knows that he has a remarkable talent. **15** My belief is that I will become successful. **16** What he mentioned was very important. **17** Undoubtedly he was a highly skilled professional. However,

he was a dull human being.
18 He was lonely. Therefore I pitied him. **19** Christy loved animals. Therefore his job as a zoologist was very suited to him. **20** Diplomacy is not the only way to deal with international conflict. However, it is the best way.
21 There has been a collapse in the international market. Therefore we can expect a fall in export revenue.
22 reason **23** reason **24** time **25** time **26** reason **27** so **28** such **29** such **30** such **31** so
Exit Test
1 buys **2** had been **3** am having **4** haven't finished   **5** have been thinking
6 completed **7** were sleeping **8** spent **9** am studying **10** were talking
(Questions 11 – 20)

FIXED FUTURE	13
FUTURE ARRANGEMENT	20
PREDICTION	14, 15
REQUEST	17
DECISION	15
VERY NEAR FUTURE	18
OFFICIAL REQUIREMENT	12
PAST ACTIVITY	11, 16
WILFULNESS	19

No.**15** could be a prediction or a decision: both are correct.
21 need to or have to **22** couldn't or wasn't able to **23** should or ought to
24 Can **25** could have / may have / might have **26** must have **27** had to **28** Can
29 needn't or doesn't need to or doesn't have to or hasn't got to **30** will
31 If he scores a goal, he will become a hero. **32** If the project ran out of money, we would apply for a loan.
33 If the nights are cold, I wear my pyjamas. **34** If you warm butter, it melts.
35 If / When / Whenever she was tense, she clenched her fists. *or* If / When / Whenever she was tense, she would clench her fists.
36 If I were you I would marry her.
37 I wish I had some money.
38 I wish I were meeting him. *or* I wish I could meet him. **39** I wish you had seen her. **40** I wish I knew the time.
41 I wish you had told me sooner. **42** We haven't been paid yet. **43** Will he be offered a place at university? **44** It couldn't have been done by one man.
45 He said that he didn't recognize me.
46 She told me that she had broken her glasses the day before / the previous day. **47** They mentioned that they were going to the cinema the following day.
48 He answered that I could take a break if I wanted. **49** She reminded me that she might take a few days holiday.
50 doing **51** to hide **52** telling **53** Eating **54** would rather **55** prefer **56** would prefer **57** an **58** the **59** (ø) **60** very **61** much **62** too **63** a few **64** a little **65** seven hundred and fifty thousand, seven hundred and fifty-one **66** January the tenth, nineteen ninety-nine *or* the tenth of January, nineteen ninety-nine **67** my **68** Ours **69** Its **70** I bought an old brown leather chair. **71** They were shouting angrily last night. **72** We will be swimming in the river tomorrow. **73** which **74** who / that **75** when / that *or* / which **76** whose **77** so **78** such a **79** such **80** therefore **81** because **82** however

4 Match the parts

Match the parts in A with the ones in B. The first one has been done for you.

1. I wish I had some eggs
2. I wish we hadn't lost the game.
3. I wish we weren't flying there:
4. If only you had been more honest,
5. I wish they would ring back.
6. If only I could sing,
7. If only the trains didn't stop running at midnight.
8. If only you could forgive me!
9. If only she wasn't going away.
10. I wish the weather had not been so awful;
11. I wish he wasn't ill.
12. If only I'd learned Spanish at school.

(a) Then he could come with us.
(b) I will be lonely without her.
(c) then I might believe you now.
(d) Then we could understand what she is saying.
(e) so I could make an omelette.
(f) then I might join the choir.
(g) We could be playing in the final now.
(h) planes frighten me.
(i) I'll have to go soon.
(j) I've been waiting by the phone for ages.
(k) I'm sorry I did it.
(l) the fair might have been a success.

5 Past, present or future?

Look at your answers to Exercise 4 and decide if the wish clause refers to the past, present or future. Write the number of the sentence in the table below. The first one has been done for you.

WISHES ABOUT THE		
PAST	PRESENT	FUTURE
	1	

6 Rewrite the conditionals

Rewrite the conditional sentences as two sentences, making one a wish.

Example:
If I had gone to the party, I could have seen him!
I wish I had gone to the party! Then I could have seen him.
If you did as I said, I wouldn't get angry.
I wish you would do as I say. Then I wouldn't get angry.

1. If you did your homework, your father would be happy.
2. If I were beautiful, he'd take me out.
3. If you try harder, you will do better.
4. If you help me next week, you'll get a reward.
5. If I had been you, I would have told him what to do with his money!
6. If they make up their minds, I'll be able to plan my schedule.
7. If you didn't smoke, you wouldn't have bad breath.
8. If you don't go to school, you will get into trouble.
9. If he hadn't lost his money, we would have gone out for dinner.
10. Unless she telephones, I'll be worried.
11. If you ignore me, I'll cry.
12. Unless you answer my questions, I will have to tell the police.
13. If he doesn't hear soon, he'll get depressed.
14. If you travel across Europe by car, I'll come with you.
15. Unless Peter comes, I shall have to cancel the meeting.
16. If I'd bought that computer, I could have done this in half the time.
17. If he'd told me there was a problem, I could have helped him.
18. If they don't get the contract, we'll lose our jobs.
19. If he hadn't bought that painting, we could have gone to Australia for our holiday.
20. If you don't give me some encouragement, I won't go in for the exam.

UNIT 23 — Reported Speech: Statements

FORM

Look at the following sentences:
'Today is my birthday.'
She said (that) that day was her birthday.
We use reported speech to say what people have said. The second sentence is reporting the first sentence which is in direct speech.

TENSE CHANGES IN REPORTED SPEECH
1 We change the tense if there is a difference between the speaker's time and the reporter's time. The table shows how the tenses change:

DIRECT SPEECH	REPORTED SPEECH
Present Simple	Past Simple
Present Continuous	Past Continuous
Present Perfect	Past Perfect
Past Simple	Past Perfect
Past Continuous	Past Perfect Continuous
Will	Would
Would	Would have
Can	Could
May	Might
Shall	Should/Would

2 We don't have to change the tense if
A a statement is still true when reported:
She said that it **is** her birthday today.
B the direct statement was already in the past. Past simple verbs in direct speech may remain in the past simple or change to the past perfect when reported.
It **was** my birthday yesterday.
She said that it **was** her birthday the day before.
She said that it **had been** her birthday the day before.
3 We do not usually change the tense if the reporting verb is in the present or future, or the verb in the direct speech is in the past perfect:
She **says** that it **is** her birthday today.
It **had been** my birthday the previous day.
She said it **had been** her birthday the previous day.

PRONOUN CHANGES IN REPORTED SPEECH
Sometimes there is a change in pronoun from direct to reported speech:
'Today is **my** birthday' She said (that) that day is **her** birthday.
The table shows how most pronouns change in reported speech:

DIRECT SPEECH	REPORTED SPEECH
I / you	he/she
we / you	they
me / you	him/her
us / you	them

We use the same pronoun for both direct and reported speech when we are reporting something that we have said about ourselves:
I said it is **my** birthday today.
We also use the same pronoun for both direct and reported speech when we are reporting something we have said to the person we are talking to:
I said it is **your** birthday today.

ADVERBIAL (AND OTHER) CHANGES IN REPORTED SPEECH
We sometimes change the time adverbial when there is a difference between the speaker's time and the reporter's time:
'**Today** is my birthday'.
She said (that) **that day** was her birthday.
Here are some common adverbial and other changes that we sometimes use in reported speech:
now → then, today → that day, last night → the night before/ the previous night, yesterday → the day before/the previous day, tomorrow → the day after/the following day, here → there this (chair) → the (chair)/it, come → go bring → take

Notes:
1 Some reporting verbs such as *advise, assure, inform, reassure, remind, tell* must have an object:
She told **me** that (that) day was her birthday.
2 We do not always follow the rules in reported speech. For example, *'I'm sure I'm right'* would strictly be reported as *He said that he was sure he was right.* But it might easily be reported in a number of ways such as,
He thought he was right; He believed he knew the answer; He was convinced about it.

---

1 **Report the statements****

Report the direct statements as if they had been given in direct speech to you one week ago. In each case the speaker is female. Use the reporting verb say. If two tenses are possible in the reported statement, write both.

Examples:
'I feel tired this morning.'
She said that she felt tired that morning.
'You are lonely.'
She said that I am lonely.
She said that I was lonely.

1 'He is looking for a pencil.'
2 'I have answered enough questions already.'
3 'I have been thinking about it since yesterday.'
4 'You earned a lot of money last year.'
5 'We were going to the fair when it started raining.'

2 Report the statements**

Report the direct statements using tell.
Example:
'I feel tired this morning.'
She told me that she felt tired that morning.
'You are lonely.'
She told me that I am lonely.
She told me that I was lonely.

1 'I will discuss it with Paul tomorrow.'
2 'He may have been here last night.'
3 'I can meet you at nine-o'clock.'
4 'They didn't leave me without any help.'
5 'I was sick for two months before Christmas.'

3 Report the statements

Report the direct statements using the instructions in brackets. (Either the speaker is addressing you or you are making the statement.
Example:
'You treat me very badly.' (Male speaker / complain)
He complained that I treated him very badly.
'We will hold a general election next week.'
(The government / announce)
The government announced that they would hold an election the following week.

1 'I don't know her!' (Male speaker / claim)
2 'You must go with me!' (Female speaker / insist)
3 'You're not stupid.' (You are the speaker / female listener / reassure)
4 'There is a solution to every problem.' (The Professor / explain)
5 'The government were foolish to make such a decision.' (The Leader of the Opposition / argue)
6 'I will attend the meeting.' (You / decide)
7 'You are in charge!' (You / think)
8 'You will not lose your benefit.' (Male speaker / assure)
9 'We have been abandoned.' (feel)
10 'War is expected.' (The Prime Minister / inform the press)

4 What did they say?

Rewrite the sentences in direct speech.
Example:
The President decided that the discussions had to be completed by the following summer.
'The discussions must be completed by next summer.'

1 The Pope announced that he would be visiting Ireland as soon as he could.
2 She says that she is too busy.
3 The Director denied that he was responsible.
4 Many passengers claimed it had been a terrible experience.
5 Burns told us that he hadn't discovered the cause of the illness quickly enough to save our baby.
6 He said he'd have a cheeseburger and fries.
7 She told me that I had been an efficient employee.
8 She agreed that he was right.
9 They declared that I would be sorry.
10 We reminded them that they had lied in the past.
11 They advised us not to say anything until the problem had been solved.
12 He asked if he should come with us.

5 Match the parts

Match the direct speech in **A** *with the freer reports in* **B**. *The first one has been done for you.*

A
1 'The petrol tank's empty.'
2 'I'm afraid I can't help you.'
3 'Let's go to the cinema.'
4 'Believe me, I will come tomorrow'
5 'I can't remember what you asked me to do'
6 'It's eleven o'clock.'
7 'Perhaps things will improve.'
8 'You must be joking!'

B
(a) She suggested that we go out.
(b) They reminded me of the time.
(c) He thought I wasn't serious.
(d) He explained why the car wouldn't start
(e) She promised to be here today.
(f) She hoped the situation might get better
(g) He told us that he was unable to do anything about it
(h) He had forgotten what I had told him.

UNIT 24 Reported Speech: Questions, Orders and Requests

FORM and USE

REPORTED QUESTIONS
Look at the following direct question:
'What do you want?'
We commonly use the verb *ask* to report a question:
I asked him what he wanted.
1 Notice that *ask* is followed by a pronoun.
2 Notice that the question form is replaced by the statement form in the reported question.
3 Changes in verb tense and pronoun occur as shown in Unit 23.

YES/NO – TYPE QUESTIONS
Questions whose answers should be *yes* or *no* are reported using *if*:
'Are you coming?'
He asked her **if** she was coming.
Whether is often used instead of *if*:
'Will you meet me tomorrow?'
She asked me **whether** I would meet her the following day.

Note:
The verb *wonder* is sometimes used to report questions. *Wonder* is not followed by a pronoun as object:
I wondered what he wanted.
He **wondered if** she was coming.
She **wondered whether** I would meet her the following day.

REPORTED ORDERS
Look at the following direct order:
'Answer the question!'
We commonly use the verb *tell* to report an order:
She **told** me to answer the question.
Notice that the imperative is replaced by the infinitive (with to): answer ⟶ to answer.

REPORTED REQUESTS
Requests may take the form of a question:
'Will you lend me some money?'
They may also take the form of an order:
'Please lend me some money.'
Therefore when reporting requests both the reported question form and the reported imperative form may be possible:
She asked him if he would lend her some money.
She asked him to lend her some money.
Notice the verb *ask* is commonly used in reporting requests.

Note:
1 Besides *ask* and *tell*, other verbs such as *beg, command, demand, direct, implore, instruct, insist, order, remind, urge,* and *warn* may be used in reporting orders and requests:
She **instructed** me to answer the question.
She **begged** him to lend her some money.
We use the *to*-infinitive form when reporting with these verbs.
2 The verbs *demand* and *insist* do not take a person as object nor the *to*-infinitive form. The reporting verb is usually followed by *that* and a subject pronoun instead:
She **insisted (that)** I answer the question.
She **demanded (that)** he lend her some money.

---

1 Write direct questions*

An interviewer (Alan) asked some questions of a woman (Hiroko). Below the questions are Hiroko's replies. Write the questions Alan asked. The first one has been done for you.

1 Alan: ..*What's your*.. name?
   Hiroko: Hiroko Takeda
2 Alan: .... old .... ?
   Hiroko: Thirty.
3 Alan: .... come .... ?
   Hiroko: I'm from Japan.
4 Alan: .... in Japan?
   Hiroko: I live in Tokyo.
5 Alan: .... ever been outside Japan?
   Hiroko: Yes, I've been to Indonesia, England, Ireland and Spain.
6 Alan: .... married?
   Hiroko: Yes, I am.
7 Alan: Do .... any children?
   Hiroko: Yes, I have a son.
8 Alan: .... do?
   Hiroko: I'm a full-time post graduate student and part-time translator.
9 Alan: And .... study?
   Hiroko: Political Sociology.
10 Alan: And which languages .... ?
   Hiroko: I speak Japanese and English.
11 Alan: .... like doing in your spare time?
   Hiroko: I like reading, eating and drinking.
12 Alan: .... your ambition?
   Hiroko: I'd like to be a Professor of Politics.

2 Report the questions

Look at Alan's direct questions in Exercise 1. Report what Alan said to Hiroko. The first one has been done for you.

1. Alan asked Hiroko *what her name was*.
2. Alan asked Hiroko ....
3. Alan asked Hiroko ....
4. Alan asked Hiroko ....
5. Alan asked Hiroko ....
6. Alan asked Hiroko ....
7. Alan asked Hiroko ....
8. Alan asked Hiroko ....
9. Alan asked Hiroko ....
10. Alan asked Hiroko ....
11. Alan asked Hiroko ....
12. Alan asked Hiroko ....

3 Report the orders**

Report the following orders using the verb tell.
Example:
'Hurry up!' (Hilary to Bill)
Hilary told Bill to hurry up.
'Don't do anything.' (Cherie to Tony)
Cherie told Tony not to do anything.

1. 'Look out!' (Tom to Edward)
2. 'Don't leave yet.' (Dianne to Anna)
3. 'Think before you act.' (He to her)
4. 'Stand to attention.' (The sergeant to the soldiers.)
5. 'Bring me a biscuit.' (Joan to Anne.)
6. 'Be careful or you'll hurt yourself.' (Judith to Tony)
7. 'Don't speak with your mouth full.' (Nicky to Joan)
8. 'Turn off the lights when you go.' (Helen to Alan).
9. 'Enjoy yourselves!' (Jane to Terry and Tony)
10. 'Call me a taxi.' (The manager to his secretary)
11. 'Shut up!' (Nelson to John)
12. 'Put the gun down.' (John to Nelson)
13. 'Give me the money.' (Tim to Margaret)
14. 'Don't shoot me.' (Margaret to Tim)
15. 'Don't start writing until I give you permission.' (The teacher to the students)

4 Report the orders

Colonel Sanders of the Kentucky Battalion orders his soldiers to do a number of things. Report his orders.

Example:
Fire!' (order)
Colonel Sanders ordered them to fire.

1. 'Improve your performance!' (demand)
2. 'Polish your boots!' (instruct)
3. 'Don't forget your duty.' (remind)
4. 'Attack!' (command)
5. 'Do not retreat!' (insist)
6. 'Cowards will be shot!' (warn)
7. 'Go to your positions.' (direct)
8. 'Don't give in!' (urge)
9. 'Remember who you are.' (ask)
10. 'Fight like heroes and posterity will remember you!' (implore)
11. 'Do not abandon your posts.' (beg)
12. 'Soldiers who have not fought hard will have to assist me cooking my special chicken dinner for the troops who have!' (tell)

5 What did they ask?

Below are some reported requests. Write what the original speaker said. Write two possibilities if required.
Example:
She asked him to open the window.
'Please *open the window*.'
'Would *you open the window, please*?'

1. He begged me to help him.
   'Please ....'
   'Could .... ?'
2. She asked her husband to do the washing up.
   'Harry, can .... ?'
   'Please ...., Harry.'
3. Jeremy asked Jane to turn on the television.
   'Can................, Jane?'
   'Please................, Jane.'
4. She implored him not to forget about her.
   'Please................ .'
5. We asked them to post the letter.
   'Would .... ?'
   'Please ....'
6. I asked her to bring me a newspaper.
   'Will .... ?'
   'Please ....'
7. She begged me not to go.
   'Please................ .'
8. I asked her to marry me.
   'Please ....'
   'Will .... ?'

UNIT 25 Gerund v. Infinitive 1

FORM and USE

1 What is a gerund?
The gerund is the *-ing* form of the verb (acting like a noun.)
She enjoys **travelling**.
Here, *travelling* is the object of *enjoy* (it answers the question *What?*) and so is acting as a noun.
2 What is the infinitive?
The infinitive is *to* + the base form of the verb for example, *to do, to be, to go, to see, to eat, to drink, to move, to love*.
3 Some verbs are followed by gerunds:
She **avoids walking** home alone after dark.
Others are followed by the infinitive:
She **refuses** to see me.
Some can be followed by either:
He **continued singing** until morning.
He **continued to sing** until morning.

VERBS FOLLOWED BY A GERUND OR THE INFINITIVE WHERE MEANING CHANGES
This section tells you about *remember, forget, regret* and *stop*. See Unit 26 for *try*, verbs of permission, forbidding, advising, like and would like.
REMEMBER and FORGET
When we want to talk about an event after it has happened we use a gerund after *remember* and *forget*:
I **remember calling** her yesterday.
I won't **forget falling** in love.
When we want to talk about an event before it happens we use the infinitive after *remember* and *forget*:
I hope I **remember to call** her tomorrow.
Don't **forget to lock** the door.
REGRET
Like *remember* and *forget* we use a gerund after *regret* to talk about an event after it has happened:
I **regret getting** angry with her.

However, with verbs that are often used to refer to a long period of time, such as *be* and *live*, the gerund may refer to the present (ongoing) period of time:
I **regret living** in Wales.
This sentence has two possible meanings:
(1) The speaker used to live in Wales, no longer lives in Wales, and regrets the period in the past he spent there.
or
(2) The speaker is living in Wales at the moment and wishes he wasn't.
The infinitive is only used after *regret* in formal English. It is not normally used except with *announce, inform, say, tell*
I **regret to inform** you that the concert has been cancelled.
STOP
Look at these sentences:
The lecturer **stopped answering** questions.
The lecturer **stopped to answer** questions.
In the first sentence the order of events is as follows:
(1) the lecturer was answering questions
(2) then he stopped answering questions.
In the second sentence the order is reversed:
(1) the lecturer stopped doing something (talking/lecturing);
(2) so that he could answer questions.
Note:
After *stop* the infinitive is not the object. It does not answer the question *What?*, it answers the question *Why?*. So although the infinitive is used after *stop*, it is the (missing) gerund which is really the object. For example, the second sentence could be rewritten as
The lecturer stopped to answer questions.
The lecturer **stopped talking** to answer questions.

1 Complete the sentences

Complete the sentences using the gerund or infinitive. If either is possible, write both.
Examples:
She admits .... *lying* .... (lie) to the court.
She offered ...... *to help* ...... (help) me.
I preferred . *leaving/to leave* (leave) early.

1 She denied .... (do) it.
2 You might risk .... (lose) your money.
3 Don't pretend .... (look) sad.
4 They refused .... (say) anything.
5 I don't want .... (hurt) him.
6 Did you miss .... (go) to the concert?
7 She practised .... (hit) the ball.
8 Do you dislike .... (kiss) in public.
9 She began .... (study) before breakfast.
10 They celebrated .... (win) the Cup.

2 Choose the correct explanation**

Choose the correct explanation (a or b) below. In some cases, both could be correct.
Example:
I should remember to polish my shoes.
(a) The shoes are already polished.
(b) The shoes are not yet polished. ✓

1. Dennis forgot to bring his wallet.
   (a) Dennis has his wallet with him.
   (b) Dennis does not have his wallet with him.
2. I regret worrying about it.
   (a) I no longer worry about it.
   (b) I am still worrying about it.
3. She doesn't remember buying it.
   (a) She has not bought it.
   (b) She is not sure if she bought it or not.
4. Diana stopped thinking about it.
   (a) Diana is thinking about it now.
   (b) Diana is not thinking about it any longer.
5. Arthur didn't remember to clean his room.
   (a) Arthur has not cleaned his room.
   (b) Arthur is not sure if he cleaned his room or not.
6. Amanda would never forget climbing Mount Everest.
   (a) Amanda has climbed Mount Everest.
   (b) Amanda has not climbed Mount Everest yet.
7. Do you regret losing the game?
   (a) The game is over.
   (b) The game is not over yet.
8. I stopped to rest.
   (a) I am resting.
   (b) I am not resting any longer.

3 Complete the dialogue

Complete the dialogue with the gerund or infinitive. The first two have been done for you.

Ollie: Did you remember (1) *to take* (take) the dog for a walk?
Stan: I can't remember (2) *taking* (take) it, but maybe I did.
Ollie: And did you forget (3) ………. (get) me a newspaper?
Stan: I remember (4) ………. (write) a note to remind myself, but I think I forgot (5) ………. (buy) one.
Ollie: Can't you remember (6) ………. (do) anything I ask you?
Stan: I sometimes forget (7) ………. (do) what you tell me because my memory isn't good.
Ollie: And don't you regret (8) ………. (be) such a fool? Don't you ever stop (9) …………. (think) about the consequences of your poor memory?
Stan: I sometimes regret (10) ………. (have) a poor memory. In fact, recently, I haven't been able to stop (11) ………. (think) about it. I think about it all day long.
Ollie: And have you come up with any solutions or have you stopped (12) ………. (try) ?
Stan: Well, I came up with a solution this morning.
Ollie: And what was it?
Stan: I've forgotten.

4 Complete the letter

Complete the letter using the gerund or infinitive. If either is possible then write both. The first one has been done for you.

Dear Mr Conner,
    We regret (1) *to inform* (inform) you that your claim for compensation due to injury at work has been turned down. Though your injuries appeared (2) ………. (result) from an accident sustained during the fire at the factory in January, we have decided (3) ………. (refuse) compensation on the grounds outlined below.
    The fire broke out at 10.25. You stopped (4) ………. (take) a break at 10.15 and according to Mr Hague, the foreman, you did not finish (5) ………. (drink) your coffee until 10.30. Hence, you were not on the factory floor but in the adjoining canteen when the fire began (6) ………. (burn). Mr Hague further recalls (7) ………. (ask) you to help him put out the fire but you refused (8) ………. (give) him any assistance. Moreover, he states that you wouldn't risk (9) ………. (return) to the factory floor and actively enjoyed (10) ………. (watch) from the distance. Not only did you avoid (11) ………. (do) any fire prevention work, but began (12) ………. (laugh) and continued (13) ………. (laugh) for a number of minutes.
    We would like to ask if you remember (14) ………. (dance) round the canteen tables and if you admit (15) ………. (sing) Come On Baby Light My Fire and Smoke Gets In Your Eyes while the fire was raging? According to Mr Hague it was then you tripped and fell onto the floor, breaking your arm.
    We hope (16) ………. (hear) from you in the near future and expect (17) ………. (receive) some answers to these serious allegations.
Yours faithfully
V. Sharp

Mr Sharp
The Manager

UNIT 26 Gerund v. Infinitive 2

FORM and USE

TRY
1 Look at the following box:

TRY + GERUND	
If you want to lose weight, try	dieting. exercising regularly. joining Weight-Watchers.

We use *try* + gerund to mean experiment with (to do something to discover the result). In the above example, dieting, exercising etc. may result in losing weight. When we use this form, therefore, the gerund refers to a possible way of achieving an aim.

2 Look at the following sentence:
*I am **trying to lose** weight.*
We use *try* + infinitive to mean to make an effort to achieve something, rather than experimenting with something. The infinitive refers to the aim itself (unlike the gerunds above that refer to a possible **way** of achieving the aim).

3 We can also see the difference between *try* + gerund and *try* + infinitive in the past. Look at the following sentences:
*I **tried exercising** daily (and managed to lose 5 kilos).*
*I **tried to exercise** daily but couldn't find the time.*
The first sentence (*try* + gerund) means that exercise has been used as a way of losing weight (and was successful). The second sentence (*try* + infinitive) means that the aim of exercising was not achieved.

ALLOW, ADVISE, FORBID, PERMIT
We use these verbs + gerund when no person (as object) is mentioned:
*The airline **forbids smoking** in the aisles, toilets and non-smoking seats.*
We use these verbs + infinitive when a person is mentioned:
*The airline doesn't **allow you to smoke** in the aisles, toilets and non-smoking seats.*
We use these verbs + infinitive in the passive:
*You **are not allowed to smoke** in the aisles, toilets and non-smoking seats.*
Note:
The gerund is often used as subject with these verbs, in rules and in formal English:
***Smoking** is not permitted.*
LIKE and WOULD LIKE
Like has a general reference (to past, present, future and recurring events). After *like* we can use either the gerund or the infinitive with little change in meaning:
*I **like playing** tennis.*
*I **like to play** tennis.*
Would like has a specific reference (to a future event). (See Unit 27.) After *would like* we only use the infinitive:
*I **would like to play** tennis (next/this evening).*
Note:
When the infinitive is used in its past form it expresses regret for an event that didn't occur:
*I **would like to have played** tennis this morning.*
(But was too busy and so couldn't.)

1 Complete the story

Complete the story using the gerund or infinitive. The first one has been done for you.

Jackie, Fran and Sarah were driving along the road when Jackie's old car broke down.
'What shall we do?' said Jackie.
'We could try **(1)** *ringing*. (ring) a garage,' said Fran.
'Oh, no,' replied Jackie, 'that will be expensive. Let's try **(2)** .... (get) it going. The tools are in the boot.'
'God help us!' said Sarah, refusing to move.
'I'll get the tools,' said Fran.
Fran went to the boot and tried **(3)** .... (open) it.
'I think it's locked,' said Fran.
'Then try **(4)** .... (use) the key!' exclaimed Jackie, throwing it to her.
Fran got the tools from the boot and brought them to Jackie who was trying **(5)** .... (find) her hat and gloves before stepping out into the cold. Sarah closed her eyes and tried **(6)** .... (imagine) she was somewhere else.
'What now?' said Fran.
'Shall we try **(7)** .... (look) at the engine?' Jackie said sarcastically.
'What a good idea,' replied Fran enthusiastically.
Fran tried **(8)** .... (lift) up the bonnet but couldn't.
'It's stuck!' Fran shouted.
'Try **(9)** .... (bang) it' Jackie replied.
Fran banged the bonnet hard with her hand and it sprang open. Jackie climbed out of her seat and stood next to Fran. They both stared down at the engine. Jackie noticed that the wire had come loose from the battery.
'It's come off,' said Jackie. 'Pass me a spanner and I'll try **(10)** .... (fix) it back on.'
Jackie put the lead in its place, made sure it was tight, and handed the spanner back to Fran. Sarah emerged from the car to see how the two were progressing.
'I suppose you'll be trying **(11)** .... (repair) it all day,' said Sarah.
'It's mended,' Jackie retorted.

'Whoopee!' went Fran, waving her hands in the air with delight.
It was at that moment that Fran, though she tried **(12)** .... (hold) on, lost her grip on the spanner. It flew into the air.
'Oops,' said Fran, 'Look out!'
But it was too late. The spanner came crashing down on Sarah's head and she went crashing to the floor.
'Look what you've done!' screamed Jackie, looking at Fran as though she'd deliberately tried **(13)** .... (kill) Sarah.
'I'm sorry,' said Fran tearfully, 'I didn't mean to hurt her. I always try **(14)** .... (do) my best and things always go wrong!'
There was a moan from Sarah. Sarah was dreaming of flying across Arabia on a magic carpet, a storm of meteors falling from the sky around her. One landed on her head and she woke up in shock.
'Have you ever tried **(15)** .... (fly) on a magic carpet?' she asked the puzzled couple bending over her. Jackie looked at Fran, Fran at Jackie and they both looked back at Sarah. They all smiled.

2 Complete the sentences

Complete the sentences using the gerund or infinitive.
Examples:
The bus company forbids **standing** ..(stand) on the upper deck.
Learners are not permitted **to drive**. (drive) on the motorway.

1. We advise you .... (wear) protective clothing.
2. The river authority allows .... (bathe) in designated areas.
3. You are not permitted .... (enter) without a member's card.
4. The hospital forbids .... (visit) during mealtimes.
5. You are not allowed .... (eat) your own food on restaurant premises.
6. We advise you .... (bring) a packed lunch.
7. Students are not permitted .... (talk) during exams.
8. You are forbidden .... (play) music on the Underground.
9. You are allowed .... (touch) the items on display.
10. We wouldn't advise .... (attempt) the climb by yourself.
11. The rules don't permit .... (stay) out late.
12. The landowner does not allow .... (walk) outside the Public Access areas.

3 Rewrite the sentences

Rewrite the sentences from Exercise 2 making the subject with the gerund.
Examples:
The bus company forbids standing on the upper deck.
..**Standing**.... on the upper deck is forbidden.
Learners are not permitted to drive on the motorway.
...**Driving**..... on the motorway is not permitted.

4 Complete the dialogue*

Complete the dialogue using the gerund or infinitive in the correct tense. Where both gerund and infinitive are possible, write both.
Example:
Steven: Do you like .**eating/to eat**. (eat) sausages?
Philip: Yes, I do.
Steven: Would you like me ...**to make**..... (make) you one?
Philip: I would like .**to have had**..(have) one earlier, but I've already eaten.

1. **Steven:** Would you like ....(go) abroad on holiday?
   Philip: No, you know I don't like ....(travel) long distances. I would like ....(spend) some time resting at home.
2. **Steven:** Why are you in such a bad mood?
   Philip: I don't like ....(go) to meetings.
3. **Steven:** Why not?
   Philip: Well, would you like .... (go) instead of me?
4. **Steven:** No. I've never liked .... (go) to meetings.
   Philip: Well, there you are then.
5. **Steven:** Do you like ....(watch) football on television better than playing it?
   Philip: I like ....(play) football better.
6. **Steven:** Would you like ....(have) a game now?
   Philip: I would like .... (play) one earlier, but I'm too tired now.

UNIT 27 Preferences: prefer / would prefer / would rather / would sooner

FORM

PREFER and WOULD PREFER
1 Both *prefer* and *would prefer* can be followed by a noun phrase:
I prefer coffee to tea.
I'd prefer coffee to tea.
2 Both *prefer* and *would prefer* can be followed by a *to*-infinitive:
I prefer to drink coffee.
I'd prefer to drink coffee.
3 Only *prefer* can be followed by the gerund (*-ing*):
I prefer drinking coffee (to drinking tea).
Using *I'd prefer* + gerund is unusual or wrong:
I'd prefer drinking coffee. (x)

WOULD RATHER and WOULD SOONER
Would rather and *would sooner* are followed by the infinitive without *to*:
I'd rather have coffee (than tea).
I'd sooner have coffee (than tea).

THE NEGATIVE
1 With *prefer* we form the negative using the auxiliary *do*:
I don't prefer coffee (to tea).
2 With *I'd prefer* we change *would* to *wouldn't*:
I wouldn't prefer coffee. (I'd prefer tea.)
Note:
There is no negative belonging to *would rather* or *would sooner*. We cannot say *I wouldn't rather* (x) or *I wouldn't sooner* (x).

THE QUESTION FORM
1 Questions are formed in the usual way:
Do you prefer coffee to/or tea?
Would you prefer coffee or tea?
Would you rather have coffee or tea?
Would you sooner have coffee than tea?
2 Questions are often made in the negative:
Don't you prefer coffee to tea?
Wouldn't you prefer coffee (to tea)?
Wouldn't you rather have coffee (than tea)?
Wouldn't you sooner have coffee (than tea)?

USE

1 We use *prefer* for general preferences.
In *I prefer coffee to tea*
the speaker likes coffee more than tea.
2 *I'd prefer*, *I'd rather* and *I'd sooner* for specific occasions;
I'd prefer coffee to tea is an appropriate response to an offer such as *Do you want coffee or tea?*
3 question forms to ask about preferences:
Do you prefer coffee to/or tea?
and to state the choices available on particular occasions:
Would you prefer/rather have/sooner have coffee or tea?
4 question forms to make suggestions:
Would you rather go out tonight?
5 negative question forms to strengthen the suggestion:
Wouldn't you rather go out tonight?
Here the speaker is strongly suggesting a preferred option (on the speaker's part rather than the listener's!) and this negative question form is often used as an alternative suggestion to one made by another person:
Shall we stay in and watch television?
Well, wouldn't you rather go out tonight?
Note:
The negative forms *don't/won't prefer* are not common.

1 Complete the sentences

Here is the weekly programme of activities at The Lake District National Park Sporting and Activity Holiday Centre. Holidaymakers must choose their preferred morning and afternoon activities. Tony has ringed his choices. Complete the sentences using the verb (in brackets) to show Tony's preferences. (The table below the timetable tells you which verbs the various sports/ activities take.) The first one has been done for you.

LAKE DISTRICT NATIONAL PARK SPORTING AND ACTIVITY HOLIDAY CENTRE WEEKLY SCHEDULE OF ACTIVITIES		
	MORNING	AFTERNOON
MONDAY	Cycling / (Rowing)	(Football) / Golf
TUESDAY	Fencing / (Judo)	Canoeing / (Rock Climbing)
WEDNESDAY	(Tennis) / Squash	Swimming / (Fishing)
THURSDAY	Hockey / (Badminton)	Hiking / (White Water Rafting)
FRIDAY	(Karate) / Archery	Rounders / (Rugby)
SATURDAY	Full-day activities: Mountaineering / (Hang Gliding)	
SUNDAY	(Cricket) / Kendo	DEPARTURE (No activity)

Verb: do	Verb: play	Verb: go
archery	golf	swimming
judo	football	rowing
kendo	tennis	white-water rafting
fencing	squash	canoeing
karate	badminton	rock-climbing
	hockey	mountaineering
	rugby	fishing
	rounders	cycling
	cricket	shooting
		hang gliding
		hiking

(Please add to the table if you wish.)

1. On Monday morning *Tony would prefer to go rowing*.
2. On Monday afternoon .... (would prefer)
3. On Tuesday morning .... (would prefer)
4. On Tuesday afternoon .... (would prefer)
5. On Wednesday morning .... (would sooner)
6. On Wednesday afternoon .... (would sooner)
7. On Thursday morning .... (would sooner)
8. On Thursday afternoon .... (would sooner)
9. On Friday morning .... (would rather)
10. On Friday afternoon .... (would rather)
11. On Saturday .... (would rather)
12. On Sunday morning .... (would rather)

2 Complete the questions

Jane has accompanied Tony on the holiday. Unfortunately she has choosen the alternative activity to the one Tony is doing. When Tony tells Jane his preferences she is disappointed and responds by suggesting her preference. Complete her questions.

1. (sooner) *Wouldn't you sooner go cycling?*
2. (rather) ....
3. (prefer) ....
4. (sooner) ....
5. (rather) ....
6. (prefer) ....
7. (sooner) ....
8. (prefer) ....
9. (sooner) ....
10. (sooner) ....
11. (prefer) ....
12. (rather) ....

Complete the sentences

Complete the following sentences using prefer, would prefer, *or* would rather.

Examples:

Generally, I .....*prefer*..... to do my own thing.

I ....*'d prefer*... to have the chicken, please.

I ...*'d rather*.... pay by credit card.

1. I .... to go home as soon as possible.
2. I spend every summer on the coast. I .... the sea to the mountains.
3. I .... talk to the manager than to the secretary.
4. I .... speaking on the telephone to writing letters.
5. I .... a short walk this evening.
6. I .... think about it for a few days than make a decision right now.
7. I .... not to say anything until tomorrow.
8. I .... not tell anyone.
9. I .... flying to going by train.
10. I .... not do that.
11. I .... a little time to myself this afternoon.
12. At school, I .... English to Mathematics.

UNIT 28 The Passive

FORM: See Book 2

USE

1 We use the passive when the agent is less important than what happened, that is, when we want to focus on the event, rather than who or what caused it:
*Two people **were injured** in an accident this morning.*
2 We use the passive to describe a process:
*Milk **is pasteurized, cooled** and then **put** into bottles for distribution.*
3 We often use the passive in formal English, especially news reports and written descriptions of processes and experiments:

*An explosive device **was discovered** in a Belfast warehouse last night ...*
*The beaker **is placed** over a Bunsen burner and a few drops of water **are added.***
4 We often use the passive in formal and academic English to produce an impersonal style:
*It **is** commonly **believed** that ...*

1 Complete the description

Complete the description using either the active or passive in the tenses suggested in the brackets. The first two have been done for you.

As the sun (rise, past simple) (1) ...**rose**..... over the city, preparations (make, past continuous) (2) .**were being made**. for the sad event. People (shock, past simple) (3) .... by what (happen, past perfect) (4) .... They (come, past perfect) (5) .... from all over the country. Extra trains (provide, past perfect) (6) .... and people (warn, past perfect) (7) .... not to bring their cars into the centre. As the time (approach, past simple) (8) .... for the procession to arrive, silence (fall, past simple) (9) ....
A policeman on a horse could (see, infinitive without to) (10) .... coming around the corner. At that moment the clock (strike, past simple) (11) .... twelve. That was a day that would never (forget, infinitive without to) (12) ....

2 Complete the description

Look at the following chart showing the processing of coffee. Below the chart is a description of the process written in the passive. Complete the description using the chart to help you. The first one has been done for you.

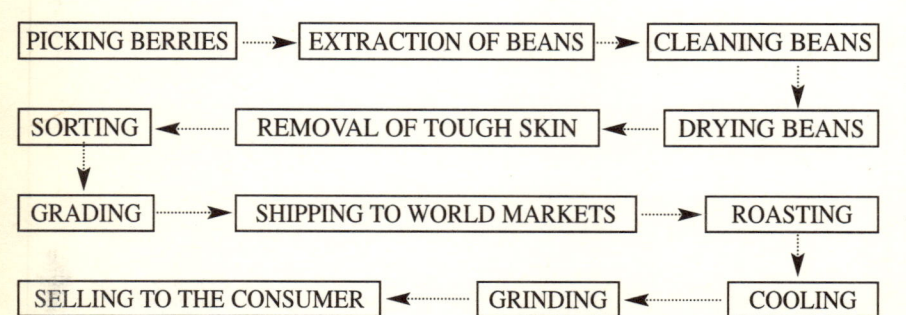

PICKING BERRIES → EXTRACTION OF BEANS → CLEANING BEANS
SORTING ← REMOVAL OF TOUGH SKIN ← DRYING BEANS
GRADING → SHIPPING TO WORLD MARKETS → ROASTING
SELLING TO THE CONSUMER ← GRINDING ← COOLING

First the berries
(1) .**are picked**... Then the beans (2) .... ,
(3) .... and
(4) .... Next the tough skin (5) ....
After that, the beans
(6) .... ,
(7) .... and
(8) .... Finally, they (9) .... ,
(10) .... and
(11) .... , before
(12) ....

UNITS 17 – 28   Revision Test 2

UNITS 17 – 21

Match the parts in A with the ones in B to make conditional sentences. Note that the dog is male and the cat is female.

A
1 If the dog isn't hungry,
2 If the cat had been slower,
3 If the dog was hungry,
4 If the cat caught a mouse,
5 Unless the dog is sick,
6 If you were a cat,
7 If the dog had not been well,
8 If cats didn't catch mice,
9 If I were a dog,
10 If the cat catches a mouse,

B
(a) she plays with it till it dies.
(b) he would beg for food.
(c) the mouse might've escaped.
(d) he won't eat his dinner.
(e) who would?
(f) she'd play with it till it was dead.
(g) he will eat his dinner.
(h) you would eat mice.
(i) he wouldn't have eaten his dinner.
(j) I wouldn't eat that food either.

GENERAL HABIT	
EXCEPTION	
FUTURE POSSIBILITY	
IMPOSSIBLE/ UNTRUE PRESENT	
IMPOSSIBLE/ UNTRUE PAST	

Look at the sentences 1–10 above and choose the use each one shows. Write the number of the sentence in the table above.

UNIT 22

Make wishes. Each time the subject is I.

11 I / be / in Chicago (wish about the present)
12 we / have / a New Year's celebration (wish about the future)
13 he / be / richer (wish about the past)
14 I / go / Australia (wish about the future)
15 they / come (wish about the past)

UNITS 23 – 27

A *Report the direct statements and questions as if they were made to you yesterday at your work place. You are now at home.*

16 I don't love him.
    (Female speaker: reporting verb = *tell*)
17 She has been working very hard today.
    (Male speaker: reporting verb = *say*)
18 Are you coming to the office party next week?
    (Male speaker: reporting verb = *ask*)
19 What's your name?
    (The new manager: reporting verb = *wonder*)
20 You can do it tomorrow.
    (Female speaker: reporting verb = *assure*)

B *Write the reported sentences in direct speech.*

21 He asked her if she would like to dance.
22 He begged her to help him.
23 He insisted that I marry his daughter.
24 She announced that she could do as she liked.
25 She reminded him not to forget their arrangement.

C *Fill in the gaps with either the gerund or the infinitive of the verb in brackets. If both are possible, write both.*

26 Would you like ………. (do) me a favour?
27 He tried ………. (kill) me!
28 ………. (take) photographs is not permitted.
29 She stopped ………. (eat) her sandwich.
30 I won't forget ………. (meet) her yesterday.

D *Fill in the gaps with* prefer, would prefer *or* would rather *to express preferences.*

31 I …………… watching football to watching rugby.
32 I ………. stay at home than go out.
33 I ………. to work through my break, on this occasion.
34 I ………. it if you came back later.
35 I ………. not sit next to him.

UNIT 28

Put the active sentences into the passive.

36 Emily Bronte wrote Wuthering Heights.
37 The company made a lot of money on the stock market.
38 We haven't completed the report.
39 The workmen had already removed the rubbish.
40 They couldn't find the key anywhere.

UNIT 29 Articles: *the / a / an / zero article (Ø)*

FORM

The definite article is *the*.
The indefinite article is *a* before consonants (*a* book) and *an* before vowels (*an* apple).
The zero article (ø) is a name given to the absence of an article: when there is no *a*, *an* or *the*.

Note:
Consonant here refers to the sound, not to the letter: (e.g. a union, a*n* honour).

USE

THE DEFINITE ARTICLE
1 We can use the definite article before any noun, singular, plural or uncountable:
*I picked up **the book**.*
*I watched **the ladies** leave.*
*Was **the information** correct?*
2 We use the definite article when we refer to something or someone that has already been mentioned:
*An old man fell down the stairs and died ... **The** old man was Jack Tripper.*
3 We use the definite article when we specify (or define) the person or thing we are talking about:
*Two things happened on **the night** of our wedding.*
*Please will **the person** who wrote this stand up?.*
4 We use the definite article in the superlative:
*She was **the most intelligent** person I had ever met.*
5 We use the definite article to refer to something of which there is only one in the world or in a specific place:
***The moon** was very bright that night.*
***The school** was closed.*
6 We sometimes use the definite article to make a generalization:
***The** tiger is a magnificent animal.*
Here **the** refers to the species in general, not a particular one. This is a very formal use found especially in technical and scientific English.

THE INDEFINITE ARTICLE
1 We can only use the indefinite article before singular countable nouns:
*I picked up **a** book.*
2 We use the indefinite article when we mention someone or something for the first time:
***An** old man fell down the stairs and died ...*
3 We use the indefinite article after the verb *be* to talk about jobs and professions:
*She's **an architect**.*
4 We use the indefinite article after *What*, *such* and *quite* when followed by singular countable nouns:
***What a** lovely **day**!*
*It's **such a** pretty **tune**.*
*It was **quite an** interesting **programme**.*

THE ZERO ARTICLE
1 We do not use an article when we make a generalization using uncountable or plural nouns:
***Sugar** is sweet.*
***Tigers** are magnificent animals.*
But note that if we specify, we must use the definite article:
***The sugar** in that bowl is nearly finished.*
***The tigers** in Siberia are under threat from hunters.*
2 We do not use an article after *what*, *such* and *quite* when followed by plural and uncountable nouns:
***What** wonderful **weather**!*
***What** lovely **people**!*
*That's **such** delicious **chocolate**.*
*These are **such** easy **exercises**.*
*This is **quite** useful **information**.*
*They are **quite** good **neighbours**.*

1 Fill in the gaps

Fill in the gaps with a, an, the *or the zero article. If there is no article give the first word a capital letter. The first one has been done for you.*

1 ...*A*.... cat has nine lives.
2 .... people are strange.
3 .... people next door are strange.
4 .... odd thing happened today.
5 .... butterflies are such beautiful insects.
6 .... elephants at London Zoo have a baby.
7 .... elephants are the largest land mammals.
8 .... elephant is the largest land mammal.
9 .... sun rises at 6 a.m. in March and September.
10 .... water boils at 100°C at sea level.
11 .... blackboard needs cleaning.
12 .... letter arrived for you this morning.

2 Fill in the gaps

Fill in the gaps with a, an *or* the.

1. My friend's daughter had .... accident.
2. Laurel and Hardy made .... funniest films I've ever seen.
3. The Earth is .... only planet in our solar system with life.
4. This is not .... first book I've ever written.
5. That man with a camera is .... photographer.
6. We don't like .... plans for the new ring road.
7. Please put the eggs in .... fridge.
8. Please answer .... telephone.
9. I've had .... brilliant idea.
10. Please explain .... problem.
11. Nobody likes .... liar.
12. It seems that .... new moon has been discovered round Jupiter.

3 Fill in the gaps

Fill in the gaps with such *or* such a(n).
Example:
It's ..*such a*... long way to Tipperary.

1. They're .... naughty children.
2. It's .... strong wind I can hardly stand.
3. This is .... hard work.
4. We had .... terrible holiday.
5. It's a pity she's .... unpleasant girl.
6. It's .... awful weather.

4 Fill in the gaps

Fill in the gaps with quite *or* quite a(n)
Example:
This is ..*quite*.... useful advice.

1. That's .... good idea.
2. These are .... easy sums.
3. It's .... pleasant weather for the time of year.
4. This is .... a good photo of you.
5. Those were .... exciting times.
6. It was .... lot of fun.
7. That was .... nasty thing to say.
8. The film was .... sad, really.

5 Fill in the gaps

Fill in the gaps with What *or* What a(n).
Example:
..*What an*. amazing film!

1. .... strange dream!
2. .... excellent exam results!
3. .... odd couple!
4. .... beautiful countryside!
5. .... courage!
6. .... hero!
7. .... rubbish!

6 Fill in the gaps

Fill in the gaps in the passage with a, an, the *or the zero article (ø). The first three have been done for you.*

George Grosz was (1) ...*an*..... artist. He was born in (2) ..*(ø)*..... Germany in 1893. He studied in Dresden and went on to set up (3) ...*the*.... Berlin Dada group in 1918. He was famous for painting (4) .... pictures criticizing (5) .... government and (6) .... military. His works express (7) .... strong dislike of (8) .... authority and caused him to be fined on many occasions.

In 1918 he was fined for insulting (9) .... German army and in 1923 for (10) .... moral offence. In 1928 he was fined for (11) .... insulting God. It was clear that he would not have survived long under (12) .... Nazi government and he was one of (13) .... first artists to flee his native land. He went to (14) .... USA where he became (15) .... naturalized citizen in 1938. He died in 1959. His works still stun and shock today and can be seen in (16) .... number of galleries around (17) .... world. At (18) .... Tate Gallery in London you can see Suicide (1916) amongst (19) .... others. He was one of (20) .... finest German artists of his era.

UNIT 30 much / many ; very / too

USE

MUCH and MANY (quantifiers)
We use *much* and *many* before nouns:
She hasn't got **much** money.
Many people live in New York.
From these examples we can see that *many* is used before (plural) countable nouns, *much* before uncountable nouns.
Note:
1 *Many* can be used in positive statements, negatives and questions. *Much* is commonly used in negatives and questions. It is rarely used in positive statements. We use *a lot of* instead:
She has **much** money. (x)
She has **a lot of** money.
A lot of can also be used before countable nouns:
A lot of people live in New York.
2 Some nouns can be used in an uncountable and a countable sense. Look at the following sentences:
There wasn't **much** powder in the box.
Many different powders are marketed by the soap companies.
Notice that the noun is used in the singular with *much* (powder), and in the plural with *many* (powders).
TOO v. VERY (intensifiers)
We use *very* and *too* before adjectives and adverbs:
The painting is **very** big.
The painting is **too** big.
Very just intensifies (makes stronger) the adjective or adverb – its meaning is neutral. But *too* is always negative in meaning. In the two examples above, the first just describes the painting and doesn't suggest that the size of the painting is right or wrong. The second suggests that the size of the painting is not satisfactory and we could say:

The painting is **too** big to fit into the room!
We can also see the difference between *very* and *too* in:
Julie talks **very** quickly.
Julie talks **too** quickly.
The first example is a statement of fact which just describes how Julie talks. The second has a negative meaning – there is a problem about the fact. We could say:
Julie talks **too** quickly – I don't understand a word she is saying.
VERY and TOO before MUCH and MANY
Very and *too* can be used before *much* and *many*:
Very many people live in New York.
Too many people live in New York.
She doesn't have **very much** money.
She has **too much** money.
Note:
The example above shows the negative meaning of *too*: here *much* can be used in a positive statement because the *too* gives it a negative meaning.
MUCH before TOO
Much can be used before *too*.
The painting is **much too** big.
Note:
We use *much too* to modify adjectives and adverbs, but we use *too much* (and *too many / very much / very many*) to modify nouns.

1 Fill in the gaps

Fill the gaps with much *or* many. *If this is not possible put* a lot of.
Example:
Greece has ..*many*.. islands.

1 Is there .... sugar left?
2 How .... species of birds exist?
3 There are .... castles in Scotland.
4 There is .... information about transport.
5 Do you have .... worries about the future?
6 How .... water should I add?
7 He didn't eat .... dinner.
8 There has been .... interest in the project.
9 If deforestation continues, not .... trees will survive the end of the century.
10 If we continue to cut down trees, not .... tropical rain forest will remain at the end of the century.
11 There isn't .... chance of success.
12 There aren't .... chances of winning.

2 Match the sentences

The sentences in **A** *are in pairs. Look carefully at each sentence in the pair and then match each one with a sentence in* **B**. *The first pair have been done for you.*

A
1. Sarah has a lot of money.
2. John thinks Sarah should have less.
3. Roger gives people lots of things.
4. His wife thinks that he shouldn't.
5. Cynthia can't bear the heat.
6. It is 35°C outside.
7. Paula is frightened by Enrique's driving.
8. Enrique often drives at 100 m.p.h.
9. Many men find Gail attractive.
10. This worries her husband.
11. Detective Jones spends a lot of time on details.
12. His boss thinks he should work faster.

B
(a) He's too generous.
(b) He drives very fast.
(c) She's too rich.
(d) She's very beautiful.
(e) He's very generous.
(f) She's very rich.
(g) He proceeds very carefully.
(h) She's too beautiful.
(i) He drives too fast.
(j) It's very hot.
(k) He proceeds too carefully.
(l) It's too hot.

3 Fill in the gaps

Fill in the gaps with many, much *or* very.
Examples:
Our cat is ..*very*... fat.
..*Many*.. children enjoy eating sweets.
We don't have .*much*.. hope of a victory.

1. Sweets are ………. bad for your teeth.
2. Are there ………. seats left on the train?
3. There wasn't ………. rain this week.
4. The bus is ………. crowded.
5. I'm ………. busy.
6. He hasn't got ………. sense.
7. ………. of us disagree with the decision.
8. We are ………. proud of you.
9. I don't have ………. free time.
10. It is a ………. important meeting.
11. Will there be ………. managers present?
12. She is a ………. senior manager.

4 Fill in the gaps

Fill in the gaps with too many, too much *or* much too.
Examples:
Shut up! You're making *too much*. noise!
Tokyo's so busy! *Too many*. people live there.
She's *much too*. clever to make a mistake.

1. The coat doesn't fit. It's ………. big for me.
2. I can't help. It would take ………. time.
3. I'm sure she didn't steal anything. She's ………. honest.
4. There are ………. questions and not enough answers.
5. I'm ………. old to go to a disco.
6. The police won't catch him. He's ………. careful.
7. There's ………. food on my plate. I can't eat it all.
8. He's under stress. He has ………. responsibilities.
9. He's ………. responsible to do such a foolish thing.
10. There are ………. stupid children in this class!
11. You are ………. stupid to understand.
12. There is ………. stupidity in the world.

5 Rewrite the sentences**

The following sentences contain errors. Rewrite them correctly using many, much, too *or* very. *If there are two possible answers, write both:*
Example:
He's much quiet. (x)
He's very quiet./He's too quiet.

1. Well done. I'm too satisfied with your results.
2. They are many interesting people.
3. There are much interesting people at the party.
4. Have you made very progress?
5. Hello! I'm too happy to see you.
6. Look at the time. It's much late.
7. Is there many to say?
8. How many English do you speak?
9. How much English are there?
10. Andrew is very tired to do any more work.
11. Have you come back with much good impressions of the places you visited?
12. I am very upset to talk about it.

UNIT 31   *few / little v. a few / a little*

USE

1 We use *few*, *a few*, *little* and *a little* to emphasize that there is only a small quantity of something. (Contrast with *much* and *many* in Unit 30 which refer to large quantities.)
2 We use *few* and *a few* with countable nouns:
There are **few** biscuits in the tin.
There are **a few** biscuits in the tin.
3 We use *little* and *a little* with uncountable nouns:
There is **little** milk left.
There is **a little** milk left.
4 *Few* and *little* suggest a negative attitude on the part of the speaker:

There are **few** biscuits in the tin. (How terrible!)
There is **little** milk left. (Why isn't there more?)
5 *A few* and *a little* suggest a more positive attitude on the part of the speaker (even though the quantity is small):
There are **a few** biscuits in the tin. (Aren't we lucky that they haven't all been eaten already!)
There is **a little** milk left. (Enough for coffee.)
Note:
With *only* we use *a few* or *a little*:
There are **only a few** biscuits in the tin.
There is **only a little** milk left.

1 Write sentences

Look at the graph showing sales of produce at a greengrocer's shop. Write sentences about the sales of products using a lot of, few *or* little.

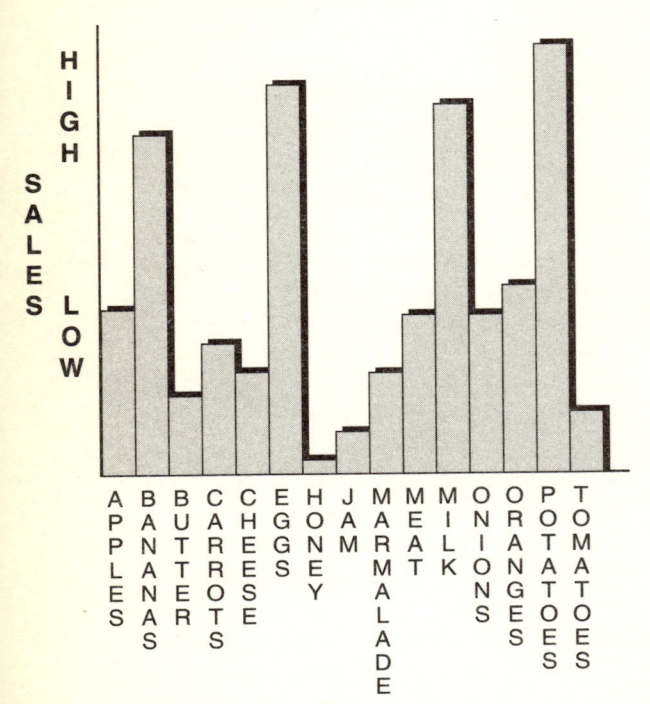

[bar graph showing SALES (HIGH to LOW) of: APPLES, BANANAS, BUTTER, CARROTS, CHEESE, EGGS, HONEY, JAM, MARMALADE, MEAT, MILK, ONIONS, ORANGES, POTATOES, TOMATOES]

Examples:
(apples)   *We sold few apples last year.*
(bananas)   *We sold a lot of bananas last year.*
(butter)   *We sold little butter last year.*

1 (carrots) ....
2 (cheese) ....
3 (eggs) ....
4 (honey) ....
5 (jam) ....
6 (marmalade) ....
7 (meat) ....
8 (milk) ....
9 (onions) ....
10 (oranges) ....
11 (potatoes) ....
12 (tomatoes) ....

2 Rewrite the sentences

Fill in the gaps with much *or* many *and then rewrite the following sentences with* few *or* little:
Example:
There weren't ..*many*... people present.
There were few people present.
There wasn't ..*much*... interest in the game.
There was little interest in the game.

1 We don't have .... space.
2 The President hasn't got .... reliable advisors.
3 There aren't .... exciting things to do here.
4 There wasn't .... pie for pudding.
5 I don't know .... rich people.
6 The General wasn't informed on .... occasions.
7 There hasn't been .... enthusiasm for my ideas.

8   I haven't got .... comfort.
9   There haven't been .... changes in recent years.
10 There is not .... activity in the winter.

3 Fill in the gaps

Fill in the gaps with a few *or* a little
Examples:
I drink *a little* coffee every day.
I drink *a few* cups of coffee every day.

1   Could I have .... meat?
2   Could I have .... slices of meat?
3   I spend .... dollars every day.
4   I spend .... money every day.
5   There is only .... traffic ahead.
6   There are .... traffic problems today.
7   How many do you have? Quite ....
8   How much do you have? Just ....
9   Have you got .... left? Not much!
10 Have you got .... left? Not many.

4 Fill in the gaps

Fill in the gaps with few, a few, little *or* a little.
Examples:
I don't like her. She's got *few* good characteristics.
I know she isn't perfect, but she's got *a few* good characteristics.

1   Many people were invited to the party but .... came.
2   We didn't think anyone would come but .... people did.
3   I love fine weather. Thank God there's been .... rain this summer.
4   The farmers are not happy. The crops need .... rain to grow, and there hasn't been any.
5   I've got .... money. How wonderful!
6   I've got .... money. How awful!
7   You'll be pleased to learn I've got .... ideas about what to do next.
8   Unfortunately I've got .... ideas about what to do next.
9   .... students attended the lecture even though it took place during the holiday period.
10 .... students attended the lecture even though it had been advertised for weeks.

5 Idiomatic English**

Never in the field of human conflict was so **much** *owed by so* **many** *to so* **few**.
(Winston Churchill thanking the airmen who fought in the Battle of Britain on behalf of the British people, August 1940)

Look at the following proverbs, expressions and famous quotations containing few, a few, little, a little, many *and* much. *Below these expressions are definitions of their meaning. Match the expression to the definition by writing a letter next to the expression. The first one has been done for you.*

EXPRESSIONS:

1   Many are called but few are chosen.   (*c*)
2   Little things please little minds.   ( )
3   Many hands make light work.   ( )
4   A little of what you fancy does you good.   ( )
5   They are few and far between.   ( )
6   A little knowledge is a dangerous thing.   ( )
7   Much ado [fuss] about nothing!   ( )
8   There's many a true word spoken in jest [joke]. ( )
9   A few good men and true.   ( )
10 Great oaks [large trees] from little acorns [fruit of the oak tree] grow. ( )

DEFINITIONS

(a) If lots of people work together the work will be finished quickly and easily.
(b) There is a lot of fuss (trouble / problems) over something that is not important at all.
(c) Many people have the opportunity to do the right thing, but few take the opportunity (and so become worthy of approval.)
(d) Things that are foolish or unimportant give pleasure to foolish people.
(e) Not many exist.
(f) It is a good thing to indulge your pleasures occasionally.
(g) Important things may start in a small way.
(h) A description of the jury system of legal justice.
(i) It is not enough to know only a little about something: the consequences can be disastrous. (It is better to know a lot, or nothing at all, than think the small amount you know is enough.)
(j) People often tell the truth when they make jokes.

UNIT 32 Numbers

FORM and USE

The following tables contain the cardinal and ordinal numbers:

	CARDINAL	ORDINAL	SHORT
0	zero		
1	one	first	1st
2	two	second	2nd
3	three	third	3rd
4	four	fourth	4th
5	five	fifth	5th
6	six	sixth	6th
7	seven	seventh	7th
8	eight	eighth	8th
9	nine	ninth	9th
10	ten	tenth	10th
11	eleven	eleventh	11th
12	twelve	twelfth	12th
13	thirteen	thirteenth	13th
14	fourteen	fourteenth	14th
15	fifteen	fifteenth	15th
16	sixteen	sixteenth	16th
17	seventeen	seventeenth	17th
18	eighteen	eighteenth	18th
19	nineteen	nineteenth	19th
20	twenty	twentieth	20th

	CARDINAL	ORDINAL
21	twenty-one	twenty-first
22	twenty-two	twenty-second
30	thirty	thirtieth
40	forty	fortieth
50	fifty	fiftieth
60	sixty	sixtieth
70	seventy	seventieth
80	eighty	eightieth
90	ninety	ninetieth
100	a/one hundred	a/one hundredth
1,000	a/one thousand	a/one thousandth
1,000,000	a/one million	a/one millionth

1 We usually pronounce 0 as nought in British English and as zero in American English.
2 The words hundred, thousand and million do not take a plural (s) in specific numbers:
*There are **three hundred and sixty-five** days in a year.*
***Twenty thousand** people live in my village.*
*The bag contains **five million** pounds.*
They do take plurals when used in a less definite way:
*I've done it **hundreds** of times already.*
***Thousands** of people live in my city.*
*There are **millions** of dollars to be made.*

c. The words hundred, thousand and million need a determiner when talking about one unit, usually *a* but sometimes *one* (for emphasis or contrast):
*I earn **a** hundred pounds a day.*
*I'll give you **one** thousand, not two.*
4 In British English, in numbers larger than one hundred, we use *and* before the last number if it is between one hundred and nought:
151 – *one hundred **and** fifty-one*
707 – *seven hundred **and** seven*
1073 – *one thousand **and** seventy-three*
17,001 – *seventeen thousand **and** one.*
357,444 – *three hundred and fifty-seven thousand, four hundred **and** forty-four*
400,026 – *four hundred thousand **and** twenty six*
400,400 – *four hundred thousand, four hundred*
5 In telephone numbers 0 is pronounced as oh (British English) or zero (American English). Two of the same number together are often spoken as double:
607741 – *six-oh-**double** seven-four-one*
6 Sometimes numbers between 1,100 and 1,900 are spoken as eleven hundred, twelve hundred, etc.
7 Year dates are usually divided into two parts:
1999 – *nineteen ninety-nine*
8 We use ordinal numbers for dates of the month. They take the definite article and we add *of* when we put them before the month:
***December the twenty-fifth** is Christmas Day.*
***The twenty-fifth of December** is Christmas Day*
When written, monthly dates are shortened in a number of different ways. For example, Christmas Day can be written as follows:
December 25 / December 25th / December the 25th
25 December / 25th December / the 25th of December
In British English: *25.12.99* (Day before month).
In American English: 12.25.99 (Month before day).
WORD ORDER
1 Both cardinal and ordinal numbers come before the noun (and any adjective which modifies the noun):
*There are **two red cars** outside the house.*
*That's the **first interesting thing** you've said today.*
2 Both cardinal and ordinal numbers follow other determiners:
***Those two** red cars shouldn't be there.*
***A third** red car has pulled up outside the house.*
*Someone's getting out of **the third** red car!*
3 Ordinals come before cardinals when in the same phrase:
*The **first two** cars were empty.*

1 Write the numbers *

Write the cardinal and ordinal form of the following numbers. Say them aloud to a friend if possible. Be careful to spell (and pronounce) any irregular forms properly.
Example:
1: one, first

1	2	9	19
2	3	10	20
3	4	11	22
4	5	12	53
5	8	13	91
6	9	14	100
7	12	15	1,000
8	15	16	1,000,000

2 Write the ordinals

Look at the numbers in Exercise 1. Write the short form of the ordinal number.
Example:
1: 1st

3 Write the numbers*

Read aloud then write the numbers in full. Use the British English form.
Example:
7,451,208: *seven million, four hundred and fifty-one thousand, two hundred and eight*

1	365	11	23,007
3	501	12	45,034
3	700	13	97,200
4	2,000	14	99,999
5	4,621	15	100,005
6	5,034	16	140,056
7	9,004	17	298,485
8	10,000	18	1,000,007
9	10,001	19	45,567,441
10	14,342	20	100,000,000

4 Write the telephone numbers*

Read aloud and write down the telephone numbers. Use the American English form:
Example:
133706: *one-double three-seven-zero-six*

1	435602
2	768408
3	607071
4	608904
5	600781
6	771144

5 Write the dates *

Read aloud and write the following dates in full.
Example:
1984: *nineteen eighty-four*

1	1066
2	1494
3	1789
4	1848
5	1916
6	2000

6 Write the dates*

Read aloud and write dates in full in two different ways.
Example:
1st January: *the first of January*
              January the first

1 February 28
2 4 March
3 15th May
4 June 22
5 21.07.64 (British English)
6 9.10.99 (American English)

7 Write sentences

Write sentences by putting the words into the correct order.
Example:
one / I know / man / fat
I know one fat man.

1 big / two / there are / elephants / in the garden
2 twelve / there are / in a jury / jurors
3 do you mean? / which / people / three
4 second / the / horse / in the race / it was
5 receive a medal / runners / the / three / first
6 first / to go / in his family / he / one / to university / the / was

UNIT 33 Possessives

FORM

Look at the following table:

PRONOUNS			DETERMINERS
SUBJECT	OBJECT	POSSESSIVE	POSSESSIVE
I	me	mine	my
you	you	yours	your
he	him	his	his
she	her	hers	her
it	it	its	its
we	us	ours	our
they	them	theirs	their
(one)			(one's)

Note:
One is only used in very formal or old-fashioned English.

USE

We show possession in two main ways. We can use a possessive determiner + noun:
*It's **my money**.*
Or we can use a possessive pronoun:
*It's **mine**. / The money is **mine**.*

POSSESSIVE DETERMINERS

1 We use a possessive determiner to show who owns or possesses the noun that follows it. In the first example above the money belongs to me.

2 We use possessive determiners even when it is clear who the possessor is, in particular with parts of the body:
*Have you broken **your** leg?*
*Wait a moment – I'm just brushing **my** hair.*

3 *Own* is sometimes added for emphasis or contrast:
Do your work! (Work!)
*Do your **own** work!* (Do not seek help from anyone else.)
Would you like to borrow my pen?
*No, it's alright, I'll use my **own**.*

Note:
Each, every and *any* are usually described as singular determiners which should be followed by a singular possessive:
***Each** taxpayer must fill in his own form.*
Nowadays the use of *his* (the male form) for both men and women is generally replaced by the following forms:
*Each taxpayer must fill in **his** or **her** own form.*
*Each taxpayer must fill in **his/her** own form.*

The plural *their* is commonly used in speech:
*Each taxpayer must fill in **their** own form.*
We can avoid the problem by putting the subject into the plural:
*All taxpayers must fill in **their** own form.*

POSSESSIVE PRONOUNS

1 We use possessive pronouns when we know what noun we are talking about:
Is that Jack's money?
*No, it's **mine**.*

2 We use possessive pronouns in comparisons:
*Our house was cheaper than **theirs**.*
*Mine is bigger than **yours**!*

Note:
Its is not normally used as a pronoun by itself. It is usually followed by *own*:
*The cat has eaten **its** dinner (its = determiner)*
Has the cat eaten my dinner?
*No, it's eaten **its own**. (its = pronoun)*
*No, it's eaten **its**. (x)*
Also, we can say *It's mine, It's his, It's ours,* but *it's its* (x) sounds peculiar in English. The noun is normally used instead::
*It's the **cat's**.*
Be careful not to confuse *it's* (= *it is / it has*) with an apostrophe with *its* without one.

1 What belongs to what?

The table shows what things belong to what people (or things). Complete the sentences using a possessive determiner to show what things belong to which people. The first two have been done for you.

	THING	'POSSESSOR'
1	the pen	Sandra
2	the books	Peter
3	the dog	John and Yoko
4	the computer	me
5	the essay	you
6	the idea	him
7	the holiday	Mr and Mrs Smith
8	the children	us
9	the football	the team
10	the environment	everybody
11	the habitat	a lion
12	the wheels	the bus

1   It's **her** pen.
2   They're **his** books.

2 Write questions

Write questions using a possessive determiner.
Example:
she / brush / teeth
Has she brushed **her** teeth?

1   he / put on / shoes
2   you / burn / finger
3   we / pack / suitcases
4   they / wash / hands
5   I / take / medicine
6   the dog / have / walk

3 Answer the questions*

Answer the questions from Exercise 2 in the positive. Add a qualifying statement about somebody else using a possessive pronoun.
Example:
Has she brushed her teeth?
(he) Yes, but he hasn't brushed **his**.

1   (you)
2   (he)
3   (they)
4   (I)
5   (she)
6   (we)

4 Rewrite the sentences

Rewrite the sentences using his or her, or their, with the prompts in brackets as a guide.
Example:
Every television owner should have his own licence.
(singular): *Every television owner should have his or her own licence.*
(plural): *Every television owner should have their own licence.*
(plural with all): *All television owners should have their own licence.*

1   Any winner can bring his ticket here to get his prize. (plural)
2   Each guest must sign his name in the register. (plural with *all*)
3   Every member is obliged to pay his club fee before next week. (singular)
4   Any person not displaying his member's card will be refused entry. (singular)
5   Each child should bring his own packed lunch. (plural)
6   Every officer is responsible for cleaning his own uniform. (plural with *all*)

5 Make comparatives*

Make comparatives from the dialogues by filling the gaps below. Use a possessive determiner and a possessive pronoun in each answer.
Example:
Me: My computer cost £1,500.
You: My computer cost £2,000.
My computer was cheaper than *yours*.
Your computer was more expensive than *mine*.

Me: Mr Bellow sings much louder than Miss Whisper.
Me: Ah, but she sings more sweetly.

1   .... voice is louder than ....
2   .... voice is sweeter than ....
3   .... voice is softer than ....

Me: Our neighbours' car is much older than the one we bought.
You: Ah, but their car is faster.

4   .... is older than ....
5   .... is newer than ....
6   .... is slower than ....

UNIT 34   Adverbial and Prepositional Phrases: Position

USE

Adverbial and prepositional phrases usually come after the verb in a sentence:
*They were talking **loudly enough** for me to hear.* (MANNER)
*He ran **down** the street.* (PLACE)
If there is an object they will usually come after it:
*I started my new job **this morning**.* [TIME]
If you are using more than one adverbial they usually take the following order – MANNER then PLACE then TIME :
*They were talking **loudly in the street this morning.***
It is sometimes possible to move an adverbial or prepositional phrase to the beginning of a sentence. This is especially true of time adverbials:
***This morning** they were talking in the street.*
It is not possible to move an adverbial phrase when the sentence does not make sense without it. Look at the following sentences:
*The meeting is **this afternoon**.*
*The meeting is **in Paris**.*
The meeting is is meaningless without the adverbials so they must stay at the end of these sentences.

POSITION AND MEANING
Why move an adverbial phrase?
In English we place the thing we are most interested in at the beginning of a sentence. This usually corresponds to the grammatical subject of a sentence.

I went to Spain in the summer.
Here the subject *I* is in its usual position at the beginning of the sentence and this is our focus of interest. Now look at the following sentences:
Q *Where were you all summer? I haven't seen you for ages!*
A ***In the summer** I went to Spain.*
Here our focus of interest is on where the speaker was at a particular time (in the summer) rather than on just the speaker (*I*) and so the adverbial is placed at the beginning. Also note how in this case the order (manner / place / time) is changed. In *I went to Spain in the summer* there is the usual order (place then time) but *In the summer I went to Spain* the order is different (time then place).
Placing adverbial and prepositional phrases at the beginning of a sentence therefore makes them the focus of the sentence and so adds emphasis to them. Look at the following sentences:
*He picked up the explosive **slowly and carefully**.*
If we wish to emphasize the manner of doing something (in this example for dramatic effect), we can place the adverbials at the beginning of the sentence:
***Slowly and carefully**, he picked up the explosive.*
Here the drama is increased by placing the adverbial at the beginning of the sentence and so emphasizing the danger of the situation.

1   Put the words into the normal order

Put the following words into the normal order, without making any special emphasis.
Example:
Sheila / a party / on Saturday / at her house / is having
Sheila is having a party at her house on Saturday.

1   in the past / people / harder / used to work
2   rapidly / the cheetah / across the Savannah / sprinted
3   I / by plane / will go / next year / to France
4   looked / towards the village / longingly / he
5   he / acts / aggressively / on the pitch
6   enjoyed / we / enormously / yesterday / the movie
7   they / this morning / very well / didn't play
8   sparingly / his water / he drank / in the desert
9   don't behave / children / nowadays / respectfully
10 she / across the Atlantic / flew / last year
11 The nights / come / in the North / quickly
12 whispered / I / in her ear / softly

2   Which kind of adverbial?

Look at the adverbials in Exercise 1. Put them in the correct place in the following table. The first two have been done for you.

	ADVERBIALS	
MANNER	PLACE	TIME
	at her house	on Saturday
1		
2		
3		
4		
5		
6		
7		
8		
9		
10		
11		
12		

3 Move the adverbial?**

Can you move the adverbial from its end position to the beginning of the sentence? Write yes or no next to each sentence.
Examples:
I will be in Paris in the springtime.   (yes)
The funeral was in London.   (no)

1 He threw the papers into the river.   ( )
2 She dropped her bag onto the floor.   ( )
3 He placed his hat on his head.   ( )
4 The competition is in China.   ( )
5 He found his cat up the tree.   ( )
6 I went there last week.   ( )
7 He's been in Switzerland for two months. ( )
8 We heard them play in 1998.   ( )
9 The children behaved badly.   ( )
10 They sailed slowly down the river.   ( )
11 She put the meat on the table.   ( )
12 The earthquake was last September.   ( )

4 Write answers with the correct focus*

Look at the following questions and think about what they focus interest on. Write answers putting special emphasis on the adverbial phrases.
Example:
Where were you last week?
I / in London / was / last week
Last week I was in London.

1 What are you doing next year?
   I / next year / in Rio / will be
2 Haven't you asked me that before?
   I / have asked / many times / but I haven't received a reply
3 Where is the nearest Fish 'n' Chip shop?
   you / in Surrey Street / will find / one
4 How did you approach the topic?
   I / clearly / the situation / described
5 When can you deliver the supplies?
   we / them / will get / there / as soon as possible
6 Have you been waiting here long?
   for over an hour / I / have been standing / in the cold
7 When are you leaving?
   out of Heathrow Airport / I / will be flying / on July 21st
8 When were you in Australia?
   I / there / in 1996 / was / just after my husband died
9 What day is she coming to dinner?
   are having / we / her over / tomorrow
10 Where can I find out the information?
   they / will be able to answer / in the Town Hall / your questions
11 When will we see each other again?
   on Thursday night / we / can meet
12 How did you get him to change his mind?
   I / him / persuaded / little by little

5 Rewrite the adverbials

Look at your answers to Exercise 4. Rewrite the sentences in normal word order, not placing any special emphasis on the adverbials.
Example:
Last week I was in London.
I was in London last week.

6 Find the adverbials

Read the following passage, underlining the adverbials. State whether each adverbial is positioned normally (n) or if it has been moved for emphasis (e). The first one has been done for you.

                                                      (e)
Vicky was terrified. <u>Slowly and cautiously</u> she opened the door. Her hands were shaking and she was feeling panicky. She glanced nervously up and down the street. Everything was quiet. Faintly echoing in the distance she could hear a train. But the sound faded slowly and disappeared. She could stay no longer. Into the street she stepped, the click-clack of her shoes loudly booming from the pavement, echoing in her ears like gun fire. Very quickly, she bent down and took off her shoes. She feared the sound. She continued on her way barefoot, her feet moving painfully upon the pavement. Suddenly she saw him. She froze in horror, her worst fear realized. Had he seen her? She dived into an alley and pressed herself into the shadow of a doorway. She was breathing heavily. She held her breath to stifle the sound, but only heard her heart pounding violently in her chest. Faster and faster it beat, louder and louder it pounded. Could she not just stop the fear and die right now? But then she heard something that tore her heart in two. A slow, steady, step coming nearer by the second. She let out a terrifying scream, more like a wolf's howl than the cry of a human. Immediately he was on top of her.

   'Are these your shoes, Madam?' asked the policeman. 'Be careful or you'll catch cold.'

UNIT 35 Order of Adjectives

Adjectives normally come between a determiner and a noun:
*The **young** girl.*
When you need to use more than one adjective to describe a noun there is an order that adjectives usually follow.
1 Adjectives giving your opinion come before those describing facts about something:
*An **intelligent, young** girl.*
2 Adjectives giving a general opinion come before those giving a more specific one.
*A **nice, intelligent** young girl.*
3 Factual adjectives usually take the following order.

| SIZE | SHAPE | AGE | COLOUR | NATIONALITY | MATERIAL |

So if you want to use a shape and a nationality adjective the shape would come first:
*A **round, Egyptian** coin.*
Or if you wanted to use a size and a colour adjective, the size would come first:
*A **small, brown** coin.*
It would be unusual to use more than two or three adjectives to describe a noun, but if you did, they would follow the order in the table:
*A **small, round, old, brown, Egyptian, bronze** coin.*
4 We usually put comparatives and superlatives before other adjectives:
*It's one of the **finer**, French wines.*
*They're the **worst** yearly sales figures yet.*
5 When more than one adjective is used after a noun (with a linking verb) we use *and* to connect them (before the final adjective):
*The city centre is large **and** impressive.*
*She looked angry, wild **and** determined.*

1 Opinions or Facts?

Put the words into the correct order.
Example:
French / a / film / strange
A strange, French film.

1 house / beautiful / a / big
2 a / terrible / pink / hat
3 suit / stylish / leather / a
4 stadium / oval / impressive / a
5 circular / a / bed / silly
6 a / little / lovely / kitten
7 middle-aged / a / man / shy
8 English / difficult / exercise / a
9 chair / a / wooden / comfortable
10 a / dirty / blue / shirt
11 woman / a / old / famous
12 fascinating / an / new / thriller

2 Which kind of factual adjective?

Put the factual adjectives from Exercise 1 into the following box. The first one has been done for you.

SIZE	SHAPE	AGE	COLOUR	NATIONALITY	MATERIAL
				French	

3 Write sentences

Write sentences.
Example:
long / red / curly / her hair / be
Her hair was long, red and curly.

1 cold / dark / deep / the sea / be
2 bright / silver / the moon / look
3 tall / fair / handsome / he / be
4 old / tired / she / look
5 thin / ragged / starving / the children / be
6 clear / distant / the stars / be
7 red / orange / yellow / the sun / be
8 intense / exhausting / the heat / be
9 polite / friendly / the man / seem
10 cold / wet / hungry / I / feel
11 enormous / silent / empty / the Arctic / be
12 warm / dark / scented with flowers / the evening / be

UNITS 29 – 35   RevisionTest 3

UNIT 29

Fill in the gaps with a, an, the *or the zero article* (ø).

Once upon **(1)** .... time there was **(2)** .... boy called Andy. He grew up in **(3)** .... beautiful cottage in **(4)** .... North of England. He was **(5)** .... sensitive child and loved reading poetry and making up **(6)** .... stories in his head. As he was growing up he fell in love with **(7)** .... girl called Mandy. She was **(8)** .... wildest and most beautiful girl he had ever set eyes on and soon fell under **(9)** .... spell of Andy's still wilder imagination.

Eventually they were married and had **(10)** .... baby. They named **(11)** .... baby Holly, Mandy thought after **(12)** .... berries that grow in **(13)** .... winter – **(14)** .... time of Holly's birth. Andy knew secretly, however, it was after his musical hero, Buddy. Together they made **(15)** .... perfect family and they all lived happily ever after ...

Or so it would have been if Andy hadn't dreamed up **(16)** .... whole story in his head. He was, in fact, living alone in **(17)** .... apartment block in London. He was **(18)** .... unemployed, his love and child long gone, with only his stories as friends. He put down **(19)** .... first story he had ever written and smiled. His stories were wonderful. Despite all, he was **(20)** .... happy man.

UNITS 30 – 31

A *Fill in the gaps with* much, many, very *or* too.

21 She's a .... clever girl.
22 There isn't .... hope of victory.
23 How .... languages do they speak in India?
24 Jim's .... stupid to understand.
25 Do you know her .... well?

B *Fill in the gaps with* few, little, a few *or* a little.

26 Unfortunately we've got .... chance of success.
27 I'm happy to say there are still .... possibilities open to us.
28 I'm afraid that .... people will help us.
29 .... sunshine will cheer you up.
30 I have only .... dollars left.

UNITS 32 – 33

A *Write in full words the following numbers.*

31 365 (British English)
32 1,100,000
33 607071 (Telephone Number, British English)
34 1945 (Year)
35 07.21.64 (American English)

B *Fill in the gaps with either the possessive pronoun or the possessive determiner of the subject pronoun (in brackets).*

36 It's .... idea. (I)
37 Is this .... ? (you)
38 .... are broken. (she)
39 .... wheels are silver. (it)
40 Their house is bigger than .... (we)

UNITS 34 – 35

A *Arrange the words into the normal order to make sentences. Do not place any special emphasis on adverbials.*

41 ourselves / enjoyed / we / yesterday
42 did / unwillingly / his work / he
43 on Saturday / are going / we / to a concert / in the Town Hall
44 are playing / in the trees / the monkeys / noisily
45 were dancing / in the square / wildly / they / last night

B *Arrange the following words in the correct order to make sentences.*

46 brown / she / had / eyes / big
47 dirty / it / a / was / yellow / book
48 loved / black and white / she / old / movies
49 some / ancient / statues / remarkable / the museum / Greek / contained
50 I / stylish / put on / new / jumper / wool / my

UNIT 36 Relative Clauses: summary

USE

DEFINING RELATIVE CLAUSES
1 We use defining relative clauses to specify which person or thing we are talking about:
The boy **who** *won the competition was my son.*
The house **which** *burned down was Stuart's!*
2 We use the relative pronoun *who* for people, *which* for things and *that* for either, people or things. The relative pronoun can be the subject of the relative clause (as in the above) or the object:
The woman **who** *I married is Japanese.*
Whom is sometimes used in formal English instead of *who* and is traditionally considered to be grammatically correct.
Note:
We do not need to use a relative pronoun if it is the object of the relative clause:
The woman I married is Japanese.
4 *Where* is used in relative clauses referring to place:
That's the house **where** *I was born.*
5 *When* is used in relative clauses referring to time:
1996 was the year **when** *I fell ill.*
Note:
In formal English *where* and *when* are replaced by *in which*.
6 When the relative pronoun is the object of a preposition we normally put the preposition at the end of the sentence:
I asked the girl who you had been talking **to**.
In formal English (or if the relative clause is very long) we put the preposition in front of *whom* (people) or *which* (things):
I dismissed the journalist **to whom** *you had assigned the report.*
7 We use *whose* in relative clauses for possession:
The man **whose** *house burnt down seemed upset.*
NON-DEFINING RELATIVE CLAUSES
1 We use non-defining relative clauses to give extra information about a person or thing. (This information is not needed to specify the person or thing.)
Christy, **who is my son**, *won the competition.*
Stuart's house, **which burned down last year**, *has been rebuilt.*
Note:
Commas separate the main clause from the non-defining relative clause.
2 We use the relative pronouns *who* for people and *which* for things. We do not use *that*.
3 The relative pronoun can be the subject of the relative clause (as in the above) or the object:
I lived in Japan with my wife, **who** *I adore.*
Whom is sometimes used in formal English instead of *who*.
Note:
We always have a relative pronoun in non-defining relative clauses.
4 *Where* is used in non-defining relative clauses referring to place:
I have moved back to Yorkshire, **where** *I was born.*
5 *When* is used in non-defining clauses referring to time:
I fell ill in 1996, **when** *I was writing my first novel.*
Note:
In formal English we add a subject to the relative clause instead of *where* and *when:* *the place in which ..., the day on which ...*
6 We can use *which* in a non-defining relative clause to comment on the main clause:
He had worked hard, **which** *meant he would be tired.*
7 We use a quantifier (*many / some / none / one / all*) + *of whom / of which* to talk about a number of a group of people or things:
About fifty people had been invited, **all of whom** *felt greatly privileged.*
There were many new computers, **some of which** *had CD ROM.*

1 Defining or Non-Defining Relative Clauses?

Look at the sentences and decide which contain defining and which contain non-defing relative clauses. Mark each one (D) for defining or (ND) for non-defining.

Example:
The girl *who the little bear saw* lying in his bed was Goldilocks. (D)
Goldilocks, *who was sleeping in the little bear's bed,* woke up with a start. (ND)

1 The cheese, which was close to my nose, smelt delicious. ( )
2 A German who spoke English translated for us. ( )
3 My husband, who the President invited to Washington yesterday, is a very forgetful man. ( )
4 The film which won the Palme d'Or in Cannes in 1994 was *Pulp Fiction*. ( )
5 He is the singer who everyone is talking about. ( )

72

6   Miss Carpenter, who works for *The Guardian*, is on the phone. ( )
7   The film which I watched three times was *Pulp Fiction*. ( )
8   The German, who I spoke to at some length yesterday, is a translator. ( )
9   The cheese which they served last night tasted delicious. ( )
10 *Pulp Fiction*, which I watched three times, won the Palme d'Or in Cannes in 1994. ( )
11 The girl who called earlier said she'd ring back. ( )
12 *Pulp Fiction*, which won the Palme d'Or in Cannes in 1994, is a very violent film. ( )

2   Subject or Object Pronouns?

Look at the sentences in Exercise 1 again. Decide if the relative pronoun is the subject or the object of the relative clause.

Example:
The girl who the little bear saw lying in his bed was Goldilocks.
who = object
Goldilocks, who was sleeping in the little bears's bed, woke up with a start.
who = subject.

1   which =
2   who =
3   who =
4   which =
5   who =
6   who =
7   which =
8   who =
9   which =
10 which =
11 who =
12 which =

3   Complete the sentences

Complete the sentences by adding a relative clause with that.
Examples:
The children read a story.
The story *that the children read* read was Little Red Riding Hood.
A woman lives opposite.
What's the name of the woman *that lives opposite*..?
1   The plane departs at 12.30.
    We're too late to catch the plane ....
2   I gave you the key.
    Where is the key ....?
3   He borrowed a book from the library.
    He has returned the book ....
4   The fair has opened in town.
    Are you going to the fair ....?
5   The politician had told a lie.
    The press attacked the politician ....
6   Marlene is on the bus.
    Is that the bus ....?
7   A car crashed into Miss Hunter.
    Who was driving the car ....?
8   She watched a film last week.
    She didn't like the film ....
9   I passed the information to a man.
    Was the man .... a member of MI5?
10 Some children broke the window.
    The children .... had been playing football.
11 A boy lit the bonfire.
    Who was the boy ....?
12 Mrs Bates stabbed her husband with a knife.
    Mr Bates. Is this the knife ....?

4   Rewrite the sentences

Look at your answers to Exercise 3. Rewrite them using who *or* which *instead of* that. *If there is no need for a relative pronoun, write a second sentence without one.*
Examples:
The story that the children read was Little Red Riding Hood.
The story which the children read was Little Red Riding Hood.
The story the children read was Little Red Riding Hood.
What's the name of the woman that lives opposite?
What's the name of the woman who lives opposite?

UNIT 37 Reduced Relative Clauses

USE

If the relative pronoun is the subject of a clause it can be reduced by using a participle. Both defining and non-defining relative clauses may be reduced.

REDUCED CLAUSES WITH THE PRESENT PARTICIPLE
Look at this sentence:
1 The athlete who is waiting on the platform will receive the Olympic flame.
This can be reduced by leaving out the relative pronoun and using the present participle:
2 The athlete **waiting** on the platform will receive the Olympic flame.
Notice that the participle does not show time. (See note) The same participle can be used to reduce a relative clause in a different tense. Look at this example:
The athlete who was waiting on the platform received the Olympic flame.
This can be reduced as follows:
The athlete **waiting** on the platform received the Olympic Flame.

REDUCED CLAUSES WITH THE PAST PARTICIPLE
Now look at this sentence:
Sharon Davies, who had been selected to light the Olympic Flame, waited patiently on the platform.
This can be reduced as follows:
Sharon Davies, **selected** to light the Olympic Flame, waited patiently on the platform.
Again the participle does not show time. Look at this example referring to the future:
The athlete who is selected to light the Olympic Flame will wait on the platform to receive it.
This can be reduced using the past participle:
The athlete **selected** to light the Olympic Flame will wait on the platform to receive it.
From our examples we can see that the present participle replaces verbs in the active voice and the past participle replaces verbs in the passive voice. (See Unit 28.)

Note:
There are two participle forms:
the present participle: verb stem + -ing (e.g. *talking*)
the past participle: verb stem + ed * (e.g. *talked*)
Despite their names participles do not show time.
Look at these sentences:
She was talking to him
yesterday.   (Past Continuous)
She will be talking to him
tomorrow.   (Future Continuous)
She has talked to him already.   (Present Perfect)
She will have talked to him
before the end of the week.   (Future Perfect)
It is the time words (*yesterday, tomorrow, will*) and primary verbs (*be, have*) that show time.
*There are of course many irregular forms of the past particular (*come, gone, met,* etc.)

1 Reduce the sentences

Reduce the following sentences using a participle.
Examples:
The girl who is swimming in the lake looks beautiful.
The girl *swimming* in the lake looks beautiful.
The chickens that were eaten by the crocodiles were not alive.
The chickens *eaten* by the crocodiles were not alive.

1   The boy who is chosen for the team must be 190 cm tall.
2   The maid who had been given the blankets took them upstairs.
3   The picnickers, who were sitting in the open, ran for the cover of the trees when it started raining.
4   The lady who was telling the story was Mrs Carruthers.
5   The book, which at present lay on my desk, was very valuable.
6   The cake which is awarded the prize will have to be wonderful.
7   The discovery, which was made by two passing tourists, will lead to a lot of scientific discussion.
8   I saw an old man who was dancing in the street!
9   General Smithers, who has been replaced as Commander of the Armed Forces, talked to me earlier about his removal.
10 The infected meat, which had been bought from Billy the Butcher of Birmingham by an unsuspecting member of the public, caused food poisoning in the local community.
11 The victims, who are being freed from the wreckage by rescue workers, will be taken to local hospitals.
12 Young men and women, who are hoping to make it in Hollywood, often end up homeless on the streets of L.A.

2 Active or passive?

Look again at the sentences in Exercise 1. State whether each relative clause is in the active or in the passive voice.
Example:
The girl who is swimming in the lake looks beautiful. (active)
The chickens that were being eaten by the crocodiles are not alive. (passive)

3 Find the relative clauses

Read the story, underlining the relative clauses. Then rewrite the relative clauses in reduced form, using participles. The first one has been done for you.

Once upon a time, there was a little girl *who lived in a forest*. Her name was Little Red Riding Hood. She wore a beautiful red cloak with a pretty red hood, which had been made by her mother. One day Little Red Riding Hood was going to visit her grandmother. Mother gave her a basket which was filled with chocolates to take to Grandma.
  'Be careful of the wolf!' said Mother, who was always thinking of her daughter's safety.
  'Don't worry,' said Little Red Riding Hood, who was already walking away, 'I'll be fine.'
  The wolf, who had been hiding in the bushes, watching and listening in the distance, turned and ran into the forest.
  Grandma, who was looking forward to seeing her little granddaughter, was baking some buns for Little Red Riding Hood's arrival. Suddenly, she heard a knock at the door.
  'Oh,' she exclaimed, 'that must be her.'
  The wolf, who was standing outside, gave Grandma a terrible shock when she opened the door. He picked her up by the ears and locked her in the broom cupboard. Having got rid of Grandma, the wolf went into the bedroom. It was there he noticed Grandma's nightclothes which were scattered on the bed. He put on the nightgown and cap and got into bed. He lay back, laughing to himself, until he heard the sound of footsteps, which was coming from outside.
  Little Red Riding Hood knocked, entered and walked into the bedroom.
  'Grandma!' she exclaimed, 'What big eyes you've got ...' and, to cut a long story short the wolf would have eaten her if a woodcutter, who had been working nearby, hadn't heard her screaming. He ran into the cottage where he chopped off the head of the wolf with an axe he was carrying, which was normally used for cutting wood.
  And they all lived happily ever after ...

Once upon a time, there was a little girl who lived in a forest.
Once upon a time, there was a little girl living in a forest.

4 Active or passive

Read the following story and decide if the participles in CAPITALS are active or passive. The first one has been done for you.

It started like this. One day an old man, DRESSED in the finest clothes, entered our inn. He had come from a city KNOWN as much for its exotic mysteries as for its riches. He removed the small bag HANGING round his neck and placed it on the table.
  'What will you give me for these, kind sir?' he asked me.
  'Show me,' I said.
  A customer SITTING at the next table looked over curiously. I gave him a steely stare and he turned away. The old man opened his fingers, COVERED in a wealth of glittering rings, and held out the contents of his bag. In his hand were six little beans, each a different colour.
  'What are these?' I asked unimpressed.
  The man, SMILING broadly, answered with a laugh.
  'Do you not know that these are the magic beans FAMED throughout the land? The magic beans TAKEN by Sinbad from the Shah of Arbostan? You may have them for thirty-three gold pieces.'
  'Thirty-three gold pieces!' I exclaimed, feeling the anger, RISING from the pit of my stomach, coming to the surface. 'You are nothing but a thief and a charlatan!' And saying that I threw the old man out so violently that he did not have time to grab his bag of precious beans. I returned to work and forgot about the old man and his beans. The beans, SCATTERED across the floor, lay there until I swept them out of the door and into the garden the next day.
  And that my friend is the reason why you see the giant beanstalks out of our window, and why we have such terrible problems with the giant LIVING above.

> DRESSED = PASSIVE

UNIT 38 Noun clauses

FORM and USE

1 Clauses that do the work of a noun are called noun clauses. Look at these sentences:
The game made them all happy.
What I said made them all happy.
The words *What I said* do the same work as *The game*: they are the subject of the verb *made*. *What I said* is therefore a noun clause.

2 Noun clauses usually begin with a *wh*-word (as above) or *that*:
That I said something positive made them happy.

3 In the examples above, the noun clauses are the subject of the main clause. Sometimes they can be the object. Look at these sentences:
I understand **the situation**.
I understand **that she is in trouble**.
I understand **why she is in trouble**.
That she is in trouble and *why she is in trouble* do the same work as *the situation*: they are the object of the verb *understand*.

4 Instead of being the subject or object, noun clauses can also add information about the subject. We call this type of noun clause the complement of the main clause. Look at these sentences:
The problem was **a dilemma** for all those involved.
The problem was **that she had run away from home**.
The dilemma was **whether to try and bring her back or not**.
Here, the noun clauses *that she had run away from home* and *whether to try and bring her back or not* do the same work *as a dilemma* ... in the first sentence: they tell us more about their subjects (*problem* and *dilemma*). Therefore these noun clauses are complements of their main clause.
If a clause provides the main clause with a subject, object or complement, it is a noun clause.

1 Find the noun clauses

Underline the noun clauses in the sentences.
Examples:
<u>That the school has closed</u> is very surprising.
They know <u>why it happened.</u>
The question was <u>where to begin.</u>

1 That the film has finished is a great relief.
2 I wonder what I should do.
3 I don't know why I said that.
4 How you laughed affected me strongly.
5 I think that fresh food is better than frozen food.
6 That the weather had improved was most welcome.
7 What to do was the question they were all asking.
8 His doubt was whether I would finish on time.
9 Your story is that you went there alone.
10 Why you left was something I couldn't understand.
11 I hope that the game will start soon.
12 Murphy's Law is that if things can go wrong, they will.
13 I believe that the time has come.
14 His belief is that flowers grow quicker if you talk to them.

2 Subject, object or complement?

Look at the noun clauses in Exercise 1 and decide if the noun clause is the subject, object or complement of the sentence.
Example:
That the school has closed is very surprising.
That the school has closed = subject
They know why it happened.
why it happened = object
The question was where to begin.
where to begin = complement

3 Join the sentences

Join the following pairs of sentences using a noun clause.
Example:
I was late. This made her very angry.
That .. *I was late made her very angry* ..

1 The audience were bored. This upset the actors a great deal.
   That ....
2 The money was hidden. The location was a secret.
   Where......................

3 She is the cleverest student in the class. She knows this.
   She knows ....
4 The product didn't sell. This meant the company lost money.
   That ....
5 How to climb down without ropes. This was the problem.
   The problem ....
6 I was taking a risk. I realized this.
   I realized ....
7 He will see her again. This is his belief.
   His belief ....
8 They were killed. This was due to bad luck.
   That ....
9 The brakes failed. I don't know why.
   I don't know ....
10 Where to go. This was the question.
   The question ....
11 The police announced something. This surprised everybody.
   What ....
12 He had suggested something. It was a great idea.
   What ....

4 Join the sentences

Join the pairs of sentences. State whether the noun clause is the subject, object or complement of the sentence in each case.
Example:
I had an answer. We should stay where we are.
I answered ....*that we should stay where we are.*.... object
My answer *was that we should stay where we are*. complement

1 He had a hope. Things would get better soon.
   He hoped ....
   His hope ....
2 The place was in a poor condition. This you could see.
   You could see that ....
   You could see what ....
3 He had taken the car. This annoyed me.
   I was annoyed ....
   That ....
4 There is important news. The Prime Minister has died.
   The important news ....
   That ....
5 There is still a difficulty. This is appreciated.
   That ....
   It is appreciated ....
6 The money was gone. It was a terrible shock.
   The terrible shock ....
   That ....
7 Help was coming soon. This was the information we had been given.
   The information ....
   That ....
8 Why would she come? I couldn't understand.
   I ....
   Why ....
9 There is little hope of success. This we realize.
   We ....
   That ....
10 They discussed something. This has aroused my interest.
   They ....
   What ....

5 Find the noun clauses**

Read the following passage identifying the noun clauses by underlining them. The first one has been done for you.

<u>What is love</u> is a question that everybody has asked at some stage in their life. Poets have sung about it, and some romantic people have died for it. That it concerns us all is indisputable.

It is a question that everyone asks and nobody answers. We ask our parents how they fell in love and they usually don't know what to say. Do you need to know when you are in love? Or is it just necessary to feel that you are in love? But is being in love the same as love?

That most mothers love their children is commonly accepted; but we are not likely to say that they are 'in love' with their children. That the majority of people who get married love each other is also true, but here we would say that the man and the woman are 'in love' with each other. Therefore, you could argue that there are different types of love.

Can we claim that love is just a human phenomenon? Hardly. Animals show love for their young in the same way that humans do. We say that pets – cats and dogs – love their owners. But is that love or just a sense of security? Perhaps that's what love is – providing and giving a sense of security.

UNIT 39 Connectors: however / nevertheless / therefore

FORM and USE

Connectors link sentences of equal importance. They generally refer back to a previous sentence and so are not often found in an opening sentence. They are commonly found at the beginning of a later sentence:
Alexander the Great is by far the most important and influential leader of ancient times. **However**, *he was also a ruthless murderer.*
They may also come at the end of a sentence:
They were very poor. They were happy **nevertheless**.
Placing the connector at the beginning or end of a sentence emphasizes it. Placing the connector in the middle of a sentence stresses the words before it:
Genetic engineering promises to bring enormous amounts of money to those who can use it for profit. Genetic engineering, **therefore**, *will attract the interest of large companies.*

HOWEVER and NEVERTHELESS
We use *however* and *nevertheless* to make a concession or to suggest a contrast between two sentences. If the first sentence is positive the second one will be negative and vice-versa:
Children are the greatest source of pleasure there is to their parents. They are, **however**, *a terrible lot of work.*
The journey will be long and difficult. **Nevertheless**, *we will struggle on.*

THEREFORE
1 We use *therefore* in a sentence to express the result of what was stated in the previous sentence:
The population of the world, and the Third World in particular, is increasing rapidly, but there are not enough resources to feed and clothe everyone. **Therefore**, *population control is vital to avoid the disasters and famines of the past.*
2 We also use *therefore* to sum up or conclude an argument:
Although it has been argued that population control is necessary to avoid the exhaustion of limited resources, this argument is too simplistic. It is a fact that the richest 20% of the world consume 80% of the world's resources. **Therefore**, *redistribution of resources, rather than population control, is the answer.*

1 Match the sentences

Match the sentences by writing the appropriate letter from the second group next to its partner in the first group. The first one has been done for you.

1 I am afraid I have not been able to fully reflect the meaning of the original language in my translation. (d)
2 It was unusual to find pedestrian only precincts in the past. ( )
3 In times of violence and social upheaval people turned to religion for comfort. ( )
4 The government were the main target of press criticism. ( )
5 Not only was his request ignored, but he was barred from speaking about the subject. ( )
6 No doubt it is good to remove nuclear weapons from the world. ( )
7 Scientists blame politicians for having misused nuclear weapons. ( )
8 I was a foreigner and could not speak the language. ( )

a However, although the opposition were worse, the newspapers left them alone.
b Nevertheless, he continued to talk about it whenever he could.
c Today, however, it is quite common for cars to be banned from city centres.
d Nevertheless, I believe that the power of the story will be communicated to readers.
e Nevertheless, I was allowed to come to the meetings and put my views through a translator.
f However, as religion concentrated on the 'other world', it did little to change society.
g What will replace them however, when the sentiments that led to their creation have not been removed from society?
h However, if scientists had not invented them, the politicians could not have misused them: it was wrong to have invented them!

2 Fill in the gaps

Fill in the gaps with nevertheless *or* therefore. *The first one has been done for you*

The French philosopher and mathematician, René Descartes, was one of the great thinkers in history and made the famous remark 'cogito ergo sum' - 'I think (1) **therefore** I am'. He applied mathematical principles to his philosophical thinking and he was, (2) ………, what we call, a rationalist. (3) ………, he was also deeply religious. He claimed the reason why he began his work was the result of a 'vision' that came to him one winter's day in 1619.
His influence on rationalist philosophy was enormous and he can, (4) ………, be said to have been very important long after his death. Despite his rationalism

he was, **(5)** ...., deeply emotional. The death of his daughter was a terrible blow to him. We could, **(6)** ...., say that he was a very complex human being, with more than one side to his personality, and not simply a logical machine.

3 Match the sentences

These sentences are all in the wrong order. Each sentence is part of a pair. Match the sentences in pairs by stating which two letters (a – r) make a pair. Do not worry about the order of the sentences in the pair until Exercise 3. The first one has been done for you.

(a) I could not have been the killer.
(b) They should be treated with respect.
(c) My mother had a bad leg.
(d) You talk about your father's brother.
(e) They broke.
(f) I married him.
(g) She needed help to climb the stairs.
(h) You need to understand the media if you are to understand the world and even yourself.
(i) You are talking about your uncle.
(j) In a relationship, women – not men – have the responsibility and physical burden of giving birth to a child.
(k) Most of the ways we see the world are through audio-visual media.
(l) I was away in Rome when the murder took place.
(m) I refused the job offer.
(n) The money wasn't good enough.
(o) He had lots of money.
(p) He put too much pressure on the strings.
(q) Animals have the capacity to feel, to think and to communicate, in ways not very different from our own.
(r) Women should be given maternity benefit to remedy this inequality and its consequences in the workplace.

1 (a) matches with (l).

4 Write the sentences in the correct order

Look at the matched pairs of sentences in Exercise 2 and decide which is the cause and which the result. Write them in the correct order adding therefore *as a connector to one of the clauses. The first one has been done for you.*

1 (a) matches with (l)
I was away in Rome when the murder took place. Therefore, I couldn't have been the killer.

5 Fill in the gaps

Each sentence below has two qualifying sentences (a) and (b) with a word missing. Fill in the gap with however *or* therefore.
Example:
I am going to London and the car has broken down.
(a) There is still a chance, ..*however*.., that I will get there on time.
(b) There is little chance, ..*therefore*, that I will get there on time.

1 Spring is the time when the temperature increases and the sun warms the earth.
  (a) It is, ..., the time when the flowers begin to grow after the winter chill.
  (b) It is, ..., the time when the grass begins to grow and you have to start cutting your lawn once more.
2 Computerized technology has allowed the free and unlimited communication of information.
  (a) It can be of enormous benefit, ...,in the fight for the freedom of people across the world.
  (b) It has allowed this, ..., only to those with access to computers:
3 Poor dental hygiene means a painful trip to the dentist.
  (a) ...., remember to brush your teeth with 'Rotbreth', the best toothpaste in the land.
  (b) You can, ..., avoid this by brushing your teeth with 'Rotbreth', the best toothpaste in the land.
4 Learning a language needs a variety of skills and consumes a great deal of time and energy.
  (a) It is, ..., well worth the trouble in the long run.
  (b) It is, ..., not an easy thing to do.
5 We live in societies where hard work is unrewarded, and selfish, narcissistic pleasure is admired.
  (a) It is no surprise, ..., that pop and film stars make millions in a few hours, and others starve on the streets.
  (b) This is not simply the result of being members of rich societies, ..., but the result of the dream that there are riches for all.

UNIT 40 Conjunctions Showing Reason

FORM

We use *as*, *since* and *because* in reason clauses, to explain why something happens or why someone does something:
As the weather was fine, he went for a walk.
Since the weather was fine, he went for a walk.
He went for a walk **because** the weather was fine.

AS / SINCE

As and *since* clauses usually come before the main clause:
As she was tired, she stayed in bed.
Since they were travelling to Iceland, they took their winter coats.
However, it is perfectly correct to place them after the main clause (if you wish to change the focus of the sentence – see Unit 34):
She stayed in bed **as she was tired**.
They took their winter coats **since they were travelling to Iceland**.

Note:
AMBIGUOUS MEANINGS (having two different possible meanings)
It is possible to confuse *as* and *since* in reason clauses with as and *since* in time clauses. Look at this sentence:
She put on her new coat **as** she was going to a party.
This could mean (1) because she was going to a party she decided to wear her stylish new coat (to impress the other guests) [reason] or (2) on the way to the party (during the time she was going there) she put on her coat [time], (perhaps it started to get cold). If in doubt use *since* or *because*.
Look at this sentence:
Since I was in prison, I haven't been able to get a job.
This could mean (1) because I was in prison [reason] nobody will employ me [fact] or (2) from the time I was in prison until now [time] I have not had a job [fact]. Although ambiguity arises with *since* mainly in past and perfect tenses (because of the time reference of *since* – a point of time in the past until now) there can still be uncertainty in other circumstances. Look at these sentences:

Since she is a movie star, everybody wants to talk to her.
Since she became a movie star, eveybody has wanted to talk to her.
Since she became a movie star, everybody wants to talk to her.
The *since* clause in the first example is a reason clause (there is no time reference back for *since* to refer to as a time conjunction). In the second example, the *since* clause is probably a time clause (the main clause obeys the 'rules' for *since* in time clauses) but could be a reason clause – try substituting *because*. The third example is the most ambiguous, as *since* could be either a time or a reason conjunction (or both!).

BECAUSE

Because clauses usually come after the main clause:
I'll be late home for dinner **because I've got work to do**.
However, it is perfectly correct (if less common) to place them before the main clause (if we wish to change the focus of the sentence):
Because I've got work to do, I'll be late home for dinner.
Because clauses (unlike *as* and *since* clauses) can be used on their own in answer to *why*-questions:
Why aren't you coming?
Because I'm busy.

Note:
AMBIGUOUS MEANINGS
If a main clause has a negative then the *because* clause can have two meanings. Look at this sentence:
Ewan didn't take the job **because** he wanted more money.
This could mean (1) Ewan did not take the job [fact] because it did not pay enough money [reason] or (2) Ewan did take the job [fact] not for more money [but for some other reason]:
Ewan didn't take the job because he wanted more money. No, he took the job because it was more interesting than his last one.
As and *since* are not used in this second way.

1 Match the sentencces

Match the sentences in A with the ones in B. The first one has been done for you.

A
1 You should eat vegetables.
2 I bought the cheapest one.
3 I bank with Natland.
4 I went out with him.
5 Edward was late to work.
6 The phone isn't working.
7 The match was cancelled.
8 You shouldn't go out tonight.
9 Spike went to Film School.
10 She left him.

B
(a) He was cruel.
(b) He wanted to be a movie maker.
(c) I don't have much money.
(d) The roads were busy.
(e) I dropped the receiver.
(f) Their services are cheaper.
(g) They are good for your health.
(h) I want you to stay in with me.
(i) I like him.
(j) Fans were fighting with police.

2 Join the sentences

Look at the matched pairs of sentences in Exercise 1. Join them by putting the conjunctions in brackets in their usual place. The first three have been done for you.

1 (because) You should eat vegetables *because* they are good for your health.
2 (as) *As* I don't have much money, I bought the cheapest one.
3 (since) *Since* their services are cheaper, I bank with Natland.
4 (because)
5 (as)
6 (because)
7 (since)
8 (because)
9 (because)
10 (because)

3 Write the dialogue*

Look at your answers to Exercise 2. Write them as questions and answers in a dialogue (using because *in the answer). The first three have been done for you.*

1 Jimmy: Why should I eat vegetables?
  Jenny: Because they are good for you.
2 Jimmy: Why did you buy the cheapest one?
  Jenny: Because I don't have much money.
3 Jimmy: Why do you bank with Natland?
  Jenny: Because they charge less interest.

4 Two possible meanings of *as***

These sentences have two possible meanings. State what the two possible meanings are.

Example:
As she was going to see her boyfriend, she put on her make-up.
(1) *On the way to her boyfriend's she put on her make-up. (as = time conjunction)*
(2) *She put on her make-up because she wanted to look nice for her boyfriend. (as = reason conjunction)*

1 As he was hurrying to the interview, he quickly straightened his tie.
2 As I was reading the book, I put on my glasses.
3 As she was watching television, her mind was empty.
4 As he was inspecting a species of rare butterfly, he picked up the magnifying glass.
5 As she was leaving the house, she took took the key from her coat pocket.

5 Reason or time clause?**

Read the following sentences and state whether they contain a reason clause or a time clause. If the clause could have both references write them both.

Examples:
Since I lost my tennis racket, I don't play tennis. (reason)
Since I lost my tennis racket, I haven't played tennis. (probably time)
Since I lost my tennis racket, I haven't been able to play tennis. (time or reason)

1 Since I told you, everybody has known about it.
2 Since I told you, everybody knows about it.
3 Since I broke my leg, I can't climb up the stairs without help.
4 Since I broke my leg, I haven't climbed up the stairs.
5 Since I broke my leg, I haven't been able to climb up the stairs without help.

6 Two possible meanings of *because***

These sentences have two possible meanings. State what the two possible meanings are. If one meaning is more likely than the other, say so and give a reason why.

Example:
She didn't tell the truth because she wanted to hide something.
(1) *She told a lie [fact] because she had something to hide [reason].*
(2) *She told the truth [fact] not because she wanted to hide something, but for some other reason [reason (not given)].*
Meaning (1) is more likely. Meaning (2) is unlikely because it seems unusual that someone would tell the truth because they wanted to hide something. Surely they would tell a lie? The second meaning is based on this possibility.

1 He didn't leave early because he wanted to eat.
2 I haven't worked hard all my life because it's my nature.
3 The children are not allowed to go there because their mother forbids them.
4 The movie didn't make a lot of money because it was no good.

UNIT 41 Conjunctions Showing Result

FORM and USE

Look at this table:

1 She was rather deaf, so she needed a hearing aid.			
2 He made up stories so that his friends would be impressed.			
3. He was	so	rude	(that) nobody would talk to him.
4. He behaved		rudely	
5. Her skill was such (that) she would surely be successful.			
6. She showed	such	ability	(that) we knew she would be successful.
7. She wrote		beautiful stories	
8. It was		a beautiful story	

The examples numbered in brackets opposite refer to the sentences in the table.

1 We use *so* and *so that* to express the result of an action or situation (examples 1 and 2).
2 We use *so* + adjective / adverb (*that*) to express the result of an action or situation (examples 3 and 4).
3 We use *such (that)* to express the result of an action or situation (example 5). This is a formal use.
4 We use *such* + noun (*that*) to express the result of an action or situation (example 6).
5 We use *such* + adjective + noun (*that*) to express the result of an action or situation (example 7).
6 We add *a* or *an* in front of the noun if it is a singular count noun (example 8).

1 Match and join

Match the sentences and then join them using *so ... that*. *The first one has been done for you below.*

A
1 He was very tall.
2 She was very small.
3 Brad was very handsome.
4 The man was very fat.
5 The girl was most upset.
6 I was completely happy.

B
(a) I started to sing and dance.
(b) He couldn't get in the door.
(c) He used to bump his head when entering the house.
(d) She had to stand on tiptoes to do the washing up.
(e) All the girls fell in love with him.
(f) She burst into tears.

1 He was so tall that he used to bump his head when entering the house.

---

1 Join the sentences

Join the sentences using *such that* or *such ... that*.
Examples:
He was a wise man. People came to listen to him from all parts of the earth.
He was such a wise man that people came to listen to him from all parts of the earth.
His wisdom was renowned. People came to listen to him from all parts of the earth.
His wisdom was such that people came to listen to him from all parts of the earth.

1 He was an evil man. Everybody hated him – even his own mother.
2 His evil deeds were infamous. Everybody hated him – even his own mother.
3 She was a beautiful woman. Men would fight to be by her side.
4 Her beauty was amazing. Men would fight to be by her side.
5 The cockerel made a terrible noise. I wanted to throw something at it.
6 The noise of the cockerel was terrible. I wanted to throw something at it.

2 Did you know ...? **

Complete the following 'interesting facts' by filling the gaps with *so*, *such* or *such a*.
Example:
In 1925 in Canada there was ..*such a*.. cold winter that the Niagara Falls were completely frozen.
The common garden spider is ....*so*.... fertile that it can lay up to 600 eggs at a time.

1 Mount Fuji in Japan is .... light at the summit that it moves with the wind.
2 The Arctic has .... clear air that you can hear a conversation from two miles away.
3 Ants are .... strong creatures that they can lift fifty times their own weight.
4 The sun burns .... fast that it uses 250 million tons of hydrogen dust every minute.
5 Rats are .... good survivors that they can live without water for longer than a camel.

UNITS 36 – 41   Revision Test 4

The questions in Revision Test 4 are about the grammar in Units 36 – 41

UNITS 36 – 37

A *Fill in the gaps with a suitable relative pronoun. Do not use* that *in this exercise.*

1 My car, ... had been making a strange noise for a number of months, broke down on the motorway.
2 The man .... lost his wallet has come to collect it.
3 Alfred, ... is busy doing his homework, is not able to come out and play.
4 The exhibition .... is being held at the Tate next week is of Surrealist paintings.
5 That's the village .... I was brought up.

B *Complete the sentences by adding a relative clause with* that.

6 The boys played a game.
   The game .... was football.
7 A department store is opening today.
   Are you going to the department store ....?
8 Sammy found a bone.
   The bone .... was the dog's.

C *Reduce the relative clauses by using a participle.*

9 The man who is carrying those papers is to give the talk.
10 The girl who is asked to hand over the flowers will be very proud.
11 Dr Foster, who is known to be a radical, will attend the conference.

UNITS 38

Join the following pairs of sentences using a noun clause.

12 The children were noisy. This upset the teacher.
    That ....
13 The car broke down. I'm not sure why.
    I'm not sure ....
14 He has a remarkable talent. He knows this.
    He knows ....
15 I will become successful. This is my belief.
    My belief ....

16 He mentioned something. It was very important.
    What ....

UNITS 39 – 41

A *Rewrite the pairs of sentences using* however *or* therefore *as a connector at the beginning of the second sentence. The sentences are not necessarily in the correct order.*

17 Undoubtedly he was a highly skilled professional. He was a dull human being.
18 I pitied him. He was lonely.
19 Christy loved animals. His job as a zoologist was very suited to him.
20 It is the best way. Diplomacy is not the only way to deal with international conflict.
21 We can expect a fall in export revenue. There has been a collapse in the international market.

B *State if these sentences contain time or reason clauses.*

22 Since my fingers are broken, I can't write.
23 As I was hoping to make a good impression I prepared myself very carefully in advance of the meeting.
24 Since the day I got married, I have been planning my husband's murder.
25 As I was driving along the road I opened the car window.
26 I didn't go yesterday because I didn't have the time.

C *Fill in the gaps in the following sentences with* so, such a, *or* such.

27 The exam was .... easy that all the students passed it.
28 I had .... hard time working at that company.
29 Information technology has .... financial potential that thousands, if not millions, of companies are trying to get involved.
30 He was .... bore that I always excused myself whenever he came round.
31 She was .... upset by the scenes of violence that she closed her eyes and turned away.

Exit Test

The questions in this test are about all 41 Units in the book. It will tell you if you are ready to go on to *Penguin Grammar Workbook 4*.

UNITS 1 – 6

Complete the sentences with the correct form of the verb.

1. He's very interested in the news. He ……… (buy) two newspapers every day.
2. She ……… (be) to Austria twice before she went there last year.
3. I can't deal with it this minute as I ……… (have) dinner.
4. We ……… (not finish) yet.
5. I ……… (think) about how to pay the bill since it arrived this morning.
6. I ……… (complete) the crossword last night.
7. They ……… (sleep) when the fire alarm went off.
8. During the 1980s, we ……… (spend) every winter in the Canary Islands.
9. Can't you see I ……… (study) at the moment?
10. While you ……… (talk), she did the washing up.

UNITS 7 – 10

Choose the use each sentence shows. Write the number of the sentence below in the table.

FIXED FUTURE	
FUTURE ARRANGEMENT	
PREDICTION	
REQUEST	
DECISION	
VERY NEAR FUTURE	
OFFICIAL REQUIREMENT	
UNFULFILLED INTENTION	
PAST ACTIVITY	
WILFULNESS	

11. He would watch the other children playing from his window.
12. All employees are to undergo a medical examination.
13. The film starts at 8.30 this evening.
14. I think the white horse will win the race.
15. I'm going to find a new job.
16. I used to race pigeons.
17. Will you cut the lawn?
18. Oh no! He's about to start talking.
19. He would do just as he pleased and nobody could stop him.
20. I'm spending the winter in Mexico.

UNITS 11 – 16

Complete the sentences by writing the correct modal in the gaps.

21. We ……… improve safety standards in the factory. (necessity)
22. I ……… read until I was 16 years old. (inability)
23. You ……… find the washing powder in the cupboard underneath the sink (probability)
24. ……… I have some more pudding? (request: usual form)
25. They ……… seen me, but I don't think they did. (possibility)
26. You ……… made a mistake. (near certainty)
27. You ……… obey your parents in the old days. (obligation)
28. ……… you swim? (ability)
29. She ……… attend the conference. (exemption)
30. It ……… arrive on Friday. (certainty)

UNITS 17 – 22

A *Write conditional sentences using the words in bracketes as a guide.*

31. he / score / a goal / he / become / a hero (future certainty)
32. the project / run out / of money / we / apply / for a loan (future possibility)
33. the nights / be / cold / I / wear / my pyjamas (general habit)
34. you / warm / butter / it / melt (fact)
35. she / be / tense / she / clench / her fists (past habit)
36. I / be / you / I / marry / her (impossible / unreal present)

B *Make wishes using the words in brackets as a guide. Each time the subject is* I.

37. I / have / some money (wish about the present)
38. I / meet / him (wish about the future)
39. you / see / her (wish about the past)
40. I / know / the time (wish about the present)
41. you / tell / me / sooner (wish about the past)

UNITS 23 – 28

A *Put these sentences into the passive.*

42 They haven't paid us yet.
43 Will they offer him a place at university?
44 One man couldn't have done it.

B *Report the following direct statements which were made to you last week. The instructions in brackets will help you.*

45 I don't recognize you. (Male speaker: reporting verb = say)
46 I broke my glasses yesterday. (Female speaker: reporting verb = tell)
47 We are going to the cinema tomorrow. (reporting verb = mention)
48 You can take a break if you want. (Male speaker: reporting verb = answer)
49 I may take a few days holiday. (Female speaker = reporting verb = remind)

C *Fill in the gaps with the gerund or the infinitive of the verb in brackets.*

50 She denied .... (do) it.
51 She pretend .... (hide).
52 I regret .... (tell) her about it. It was a secret and she went and told everybody.
53 ....(eat) is forbidden in the editing suite.

D *Put* prefer, would prefer *or* would rather *into the gaps to express preferences.*

54 I .... do it now.
55 I .... getting up early to getting up late.
56 I .... a soft drink, if you don't mind.

UNITS 29 – 33

A *Fill in the gaps with* a, an, the *or the zero article (ø).*

57 She is .... intelligent woman.
58 He is .... strongest man in the world.
59 I like spending .... time with her.

B *Fill in the gaps with* much, many, very *or* too.

60 He's a .... wonderful man.
61 There is not .... left.
62 The cat's .... wild to live in the house.

C *Fill in the gaps with* a few *or* a little.

63 I've got .... books upstairs.
64 There is .... in the cupboard.

D *Write these numbers as full words.*

65 750,751 (British English)
66 1.10.99 (American English)

E *Fill in the gaps with either the possessive pronoun or the possessive determiner of the subject pronoun in brackets.*

67 She is .... girlfriend. (I)
68 .... is not very good. (we)
69 .... handle has fallen off. (it)

UNITS 34 – 35

Put these words in the correct (or usual) order to make sentences.

70 old / I / an / leather / bought / chair / brown
71 were shouting / last night / they / angrily
72 will be swimming / tomorrow / we / in the river

UNITS 36 – 41

A *Fill in the gaps with a relative pronoun. If more than one relative pronoun is possible, write them all.*

73 The dinner, ... had been cooking for hours, was almost ready.
74 The girl .... was sitting in the corner was from Istanbul.
75 1994 was the year .... we got married.
76 The man .... car had been stolen was very angry.

B *Fill the gaps with* so, such *or* such a.

77 You are .... happy to be nearly finished..
78 He made .... good impression on me.
79 I have never had .... pleasure in my life.

C *Fill in the gaps with* because, however *or* therefore.

80 I had had my wallet stolen and .... I had no money
81 .... I wanted to play well in the concert, I was practising hard.
82 I may be an interesting man. I have a boring life ....

Irregular verbs

Present Simple/ Infinitive	Past Simple	Past Participle
be	was/were	been
become	became	become
begin	began	begun
bite	bit	bitten
blow	blew	blown
break	broke	broken
bring	brought	brought
build	built	built
buy	bought	bought
catch	caught	caught
choose	chose	chosen
come	came	come
cut	cut	cut
dig	dug	dug
do	did	done
draw	drew	drawn
drive	drove	driven
eat	ate	eaten
fall	fell	fallen
fed	fed	fed
fight	fought	fought
find	found	found
fly	flew	flown
forget	forgot	forgotten
forgive	forgave	forgiven
get	got	got
give	gave	given
go	went	gone
grow	grew	grown
hang	hung	hung
have	had	had
hear	heard	heard
hit	hit	hit
hold	held	held
hurt	hurt	hurt
keep	kept	kept
know	knew	known
lay	laid	laid
lead	led	led

Present Simple/ Infinitive	Past Simple	Past Participle
leave	left	left
lend	lent	lent
let	let	let
lie	lay	lain
light	lit	lit
lose	lost	lost
make	made	made
meet	met	met
pay	paid	paid
put	put	put
read	read	read
ride	rode	ridden
ring	rang	rung
run	ran	run
say	said	said
see	saw	seen
sell	sold	sold
send	sent	sent
shine	shone	shone
show	showed	shown
shut	shut	shut
sing	sang	sung
sit	sat	sat
sleep	slept	slept
speak	spoke	spoken
spend	spent	spent
stand	stood	stood
steal	stole	stolen
swim	swam	swum
take	took	taken
teach	taught	taught
tell	told	told
think	thought	thought
throw	threw	thrown
understand	understood	understood
wake	woke	woken
wear	wore	worn
win	won	won
write	wrote	written

Punctuation and Spelling

Punctuation
CAPITAL LETTERS
We use capital letters for
1 the word at the beginning of a sentence:
The day started well for John.
It was the best time of the year.
2 whenever we use the first person singular I
I met him in the evening.
You and I must go to the theatre together soon.
3 with names of people and places, titles of books and journals, days of the week and months:
Gillian Wright
War and Peace
Mount Everest
The Times
Tuesday
June

FULL STOP
We put a full stop at the end
1 of sentences which are statements:
It rained all night.
2 or imperative forms which are not strong orders:
Come home early.

COMMA
We use a comma when
1 we are connecting two main clauses with and or but, if the subject is different in each clause:
He left home and went to work.
(No comma (the subject is the same in each clause.)
She left home early, but the train was very late.
(Comma – the subject is different in each clause.)
2 after a subordinate clause:
When he came home, he felt very angry.
3 but not before a subordinate clause:
He felt very angry when he came home.
4 after an adverbial or prepositional phrase:
On Sunday, I'll meet Anne.
5 but not before an adverbial or prepositional phrase:
I'll meet Anne on Sunday.

Spelling
PLURAL NOUNS
Regular nouns
1 Most nouns add s to the singular when they become plural:
book – books, apple – apples
2 For nouns ending in *ch, sh, s, ss, x* in the singular, add *es* to the noun to make the plural form:
watch – watches, wish – wishes, bus – buses, box – boxes
3 For nouns ending in consonant + y in the singular, change y to i and add es to make the plural:
baby – babies, lady – ladies
4 For nouns ending in vowel + y in the singular, add only *s* to make the plural form:
day – days, monkey – monkeys

Regular forms
1 For some nouns that end in *o* add *es* to form the plural:
potato – potatoes, tomato – tomatoes, hero – heroes
2 For some nouns that end in *f* or *fe*, change the *f* to *v* and add *es*:
calf – calves, half – halves, wife – wives
3 There are six important nouns which change completely:
foot – feet, tooth – teeth, man – men, woman – women, mouse – mice, child – children
4 Some nouns do not have a different form for the plural:
sheep – sheep, deer – deer, aircraft – aircraft

DOUBLING CONSONANTS
Words with one syllable
Verbs and adjectives that end in vowel + consonant (e.g. *to stop, to plan, wet, thin*) double the consonant before adding an ending.
For verbs *-ed* or *-ing*:
*stop – sto**pp**ed – sto**pp**ing*
*plan – pla**nn**ed – pla**nn**ing*
*rub – ru**bb**ed – ru**bb**ing*
For adjectives *-er* or *-est*:
*wet – we**tt**er – we**tt**est*
*thin – thi**nn**er – thi**nn**est*
*big – bi**gg**er – bi**gg**est*

Words with more then one syllable
1 For verbs that end in vowel + consonant (e.g. *prefer, begin, visit*) we double the consonant when the final syllable is stressed:
*pre**fer** – preferred – preferring*
*be**gin** – beginning (begin is an irregular verb in the past)*
*per**mit** – permitted – permitting*
*re**gret** – regretted – regretting*
2 When the final consonant is not stressed, we do not double the final consonant:
*vi**sit** – visited – visiting*
*re**mem**ber – remembered – remembering*
*ha**pp**en – happened – happening*
3 In British English, for verbs ending in *l*, put *ll* before *-ed* or *-ing*
travel – travelled – travelling

Note:
In American English they do not double the l:
travel – traveled – traveling